Annotated Bibliography of Puerto Rican Bibliographies

Annotated Bibliography of Puerto Rican Bibliographies

Compiled by
Fay Fowlie-Flores

Bibliographies and Indexes in Ethnic Studies, Number 1

GREENWOOD PRESS
New York • Westport, Connecticut • London

Library of Congress Cataloging-in-Publication Data

Fowlie-Flores, Fay.
  Annotated bibliography of Puerto Rican bibliographies / compiled
by Fay Fowlie-Flores.
      p.   cm. — (Bibliographies and indexes in ethnic studies ; no.
  1)
    ISBN 0-313-26124-5 (lib. bdg. : alk. paper)
    1. Puerto Rico—Bibliography. 2. Bibliography—Bibliography—
  Puerto Rico. 3. Puerto Ricans—United States—Bibliography.
  I. Title. II. Series.
  Z1551.F69   1990
  [F1958]
  016.01697295—dc20   89-28610

British Library Cataloguing in Publication Data is available.

Library of Congress Catalog Card Number: 89-28610
ISBN: 0-313-26124-5

First published in 1990

Greenwood Press, Inc.
88 Post Road West, Westport, Connecticut 06881

Printed in the United States of America

∞ ™

The paper used in this book complies with the
Permanent Paper Standard issued by the National
Information Standards Organization (Z39.48-1984).

10 9 8 7 6 5 4 3 2 1

To my husband, Abraham, without whose
understanding this book would not have been written

Contents

Preface

Puerto Rico's literary and intellectual history is reflected in an ample harvest of books, journals, newspapers, government documents, pamphlets, theses, dissertations and other publications. However, it has been mainly during this century that great efforts have been made to compile bibliographies that record the publications of Puerto Ricans or others writing about Puerto Rico and its people. During the nineteenth century, only a few scholars dedicated time to this task.

A bibliography of bibliographies is the most basic of reference tools in any field of learning. Scholars undertaking research logically consult them as a first step in their quest for information. However, since no extensive bibliography of Puerto Rican bibliographies has yet been published, the student of things Puerto Rican has had to search for bibliographies in scattered sources. While most interested researchers, educators, and librarians are familiar with certain basic bibliographies such as those by Sama, Pedreira, and Vivó, they may be unaware of other useful works which have been compiled in recent decades. Unfortunately, these new contributions are dispersed in journals, government publications, mimeographed lists, and books published by research institutions, universities, libraries and commercial publishers. Valuable material has also appeared in bibliographies on Latin America and/or the Caribbean. Book catalogs of large library collections also contain numerous references and constitute important location tools.

The present work has been prepared in an attempt to fill this gap by providing references to and information on all significant bibliographies which have been compiled on the following: Puerto Rico in general, special topics or specific individuals, and Puerto Ricans in the United States. It should prove useful to scholars, educators, librarians, government officials, students and interested laypersons. It is also hoped that more Puerto Ricans will become aware of the widespread interest in Puerto Rican studies that exists on the mainland, and of the significant contributions being made by scholars at stateside institutions. At the same time, it is hoped that mainlanders are alerted to bibliographical studies being produced in Puerto Rico which might have otherwise been overlooked.

Both Spanish and English-language bibliographies and bibliographic essays have been included in the present compilation. A few scattered references to important works written in other languages will also be found. Works cited may have been published in books, journals, newspapers, theses, microform or mimeograph. Bibliographies that have been published in Puerto Rico but do not deal with a Puerto Rican theme are excluded. For the sake of manageability, with few exceptions, bibliographies appearing at the end of general books or chapters in books, or appended to journal articles are not cited. References to these bibliographies can be found in **Bibliographic Index**.

This bibliography covers works written from earliest times to 1988, although a few items published this year have also been described where possible. In order to be included, works cited should have at least ten items. Several exceptions have been made in very specialized fields not covered by major works.   Other criteria taken into account included authority or importance of the compiler and uniqueness of coverage.

Following a general introduction to the history and present status of Puerto Rican bibliography, entries are arranged alphabetically in three main sections: Puerto Rico in general, special topics, and Puerto Ricans in the United States. The section on special topics is subdivided alphabetically by subject. Works dealing with Puerto Ricans in the United States are cited in chapter three, even if they deal with a specific topic such as women. References follow the format stipulated in the 13th edition of **The Chicago Manual of Style**. However, Turabian's **A Manual for Writers of Term Papers, Theses and Dissertations** (4th edition) was also consulted occasionally. Each entry was assigned a number keyed to the chapter number. For typographical reasons, no distinction is made between pages and leaves - all are labelled as pages.

Annotations are provided for each entry. They clarify the subject matter of the work, the authority of the compiler, and the organization of the work. To some extent, they reflect the importance of the item or its complexity. Wherever possible, the number of references included in each bibliography is indicated.

Author, title and subject indexes have been included to facilitate access to all references by a particular author or on a specific topic. The entry numbers, not page numbers, are cited in each index.   Readers are encouraged to make full use of these indexes.

The list of **Sources Consulted** is a basic one since all sources cited in this book were carefully examined for references to additional bibliographies.

I would appreciate receiving information on bibliographies which could be included in a future edition of this book.

Grateful acknowledgment is made to the System of Regional Colleges of the University of Puerto Rico for the release time and stipend which permitted the completion of this undertaking. I am indebted to Professors Pedro E. Laboy, Director and Dean, and Roberto Colón, Library Director, of the University of Puerto Rico in Ponce for their faith, support and encouragement. I greatly appreciate the help received at various libraries in Puerto Rico as well as the Library of Congress: the University of Puerto Rico in Río Piedras, Bayamón, Humacao, Arecibo, Utuado, Aguadilla, and Cayey; Catholic University of Puerto Rico; Interamerican University in San Germán; Sacred Heart University, and the Regional Library of the Caribbean and Latin America. Thanks are also due to Almaluces Figueroa, Joan Hayes, Gladys Cruz, Sheila Dunstan, Ana M. Ortiz, Darlene Walter, Saulo Cotto, Aura Jiménez, Conrado Calzada and Tomás Sarramía. Last, but certainly not least, my family deserves special gratitude and recognition for their understanding, love and patience.

Introduction

More than a century has elapsed since the compilation of the first bibliography of materials written by Puerto Ricans or about Puerto Rico. Since that time the island has continued to inspire the creativity of its children and others who come to its shores later in life. However, far less attention has been given to the equally important task of recording that creativity. Much remains to be done.

A young poet and dramatist living in Mayagüez compiled the first Puerto Rican bibliography. Manuel María Sama (1850-1913) felt it was his "patriotic duty" to respond to the challenge presented by the Puerto Rican Atheneum in its literary competition of 1887. Originally Sama prepared his work by citing and describing 250 works from his personal library, excluding government reports and school texts. Upon request from the Atheneum, he added an appendix of thirty-nine additional works published in 1886 or earlier. He recognized that his work was not exhaustive but correctly felt that it filled a gap and was a precursor of future works.

Sama chose to present his bibliography in chronological order to show the "slow progress" of Puerto Rico's bibliographic production. In his introduction he related this slow development to that of education and printing, repeatedly emphasizing the importance of providing education for all citizens. The introduction also includes a statistical analysis of works cited by date of publication, city of publication, subject and author. His prefatory comments in the appendix show enthusiasm over the number of works published in 1886 which he took as a sign of hope for the future.

The young poet performed a further service to those who use his bibliography by giving brief descriptions of the contents of each item, except for literary works which generally have none. He also prepared a title index to complete the book. In spite of its shortcomings and gaps, Sama's **Bibliografía puerto-riqueña** must be recognized as a pioneering work.

Almost fifteen years went by before the next significant bibliography was prepared for the 1893 Insular Exhibition celebrated in commemoration of the discovery of Puerto Rico. This **Bibliografía puertorriqueña** won the gold medal. However, it was not published until 1934.

The compilation of this work was originally undertaken by José Géigel y Zenón. Proud owner of one of the largest private libraries [1] at that time, Géigel also worked as a librarian at the Atheneum for a number of years. Unfortunately, he died on December 30, 1892, without having finished his project. Géigel's widow entrusted the completion of the bibliography to her husband's friend Abelardo Morales Ferrer. Morales submitted the still incomplete work to the Exhibition where it received first prize. In 1894 Morales died in Switzerland and the manuscript was "lost" until its discovery in the Atheneum in 1926. By 1933 Géigel's son Fernando had edited and prepared the manuscript for publication. He also compiled four useful indexes: author, title, chronological and subject.

Covering to 1894, the **Bibliografía puertorriqueña** is organized in three sections: books written and printed in Puerto Rico from 1807 (the year in which Géigel mistakenly believed the first printing press was brought into the country); books written in Puerto Rico or elsewhere by Puerto Ricans and printed in Spain or other countries; and books written by other nationals and printed outside Puerto Rico, but which deal with the island in some way. The appendix, which was also prepared by Fernando J. Géigel Sabat, sheds additional light on some of the sources cited in the main body of the work.

Throughout the book can be found portraits of important authors accompanied by biographical sketches as well as facsimile title pages from many works cited. Almost all entries are annotated. In fact, Pedreira considered the descriptions and evaluative comments contained in the annotations to be the greatest strong point of the work. [2]

The Géigel bibliography contains 498 entries as compared to Sama's 289. However, Sama's work includes some references not mentioned in the later work. On the other hand, as Josefina Rivera de Alvarez points out, Géigel and Morales cite some works which do not appear in Pedreira's great compilation. [3]

In 1910 the illustrious Puerto Rican historian, Cayetano Coll y Toste, began to publish his "Bibliografía puertorriqueña" in various newspapers (**La Democracia** and **Puerto Rico Ilustrado**). He cited both contemporary and previously published books, journals and newspapers. His notes on the contents of the items were very useful. However, the work was never completed and did not pass the letter "A."

Hailed as a "cornerstone reference" [4], Antonio S. Pedreiera's **Bibliografía puertorriqueña (1493-1930)** was the first comprehesive, general bibliography and was published in 1932. It covered works written in or about Puerto Rico from earliest time to 1930. An appendix cited additional materials published in 1931.

In 1925 Pedreira began collecting references for a manual to be used in a course on Puerto Rican literature. However, as he discovered more and

more important materials previously unknown to him, he began to widen the
scope of his work to a comprehensive, retrospective, general bibliography on
Puerto Rico. He hoped it could serve as a guide to the formation of a Puerto
Rican library that did not (and does not) yet exist. Pedreira considered that
previous works did not give a precise idea of how many publications had
been produced in Puerto Rico.

He therefore visited important libraries in the United States as well
as local private collections such as those of Enrique Adsuar and Robert L.
Junghanns. In addition, help and support were received from Tomás Navarro
Tomás, Rafael W. Ramírez, Guillermo V. Cintrón, Emilio Pasarell, Augusto
Malaret, Eugenio Astol and others. Many of these intellectuals provided
Pedreira with references to materials which he did not examine personally
but included in his book.

Pedreira's great work was the first to follow a subject arrangement.
Over 10,000 entries were organized by ten major subjects, each of which
was further subdivided by topic. This arrangement was supplemented by
author and subject indexes. Unfortunately, no title index was included.
Citations refer to books, journals, journal articles, pamphlets, chapters in
books and others. Not included were newspaper articles, manuscripts,
prayer books, municipal ordinances, reports and budgets, and by-laws of
churches, casinos, associations and other such groups. In his introduction
Pedreira mentions that he decided not to include abstract materials which
would prove to be of little help to historians. [5]

The bibliography has two sections that add to its value. Researchers
interested in studying one of the island's towns should first consult the
section on municipal history where towns appear alphabetically. Under each
is a list of relevant sources. Similarily, for the study of important Puerto
Ricans one might wish to consult the Puerto Rican biography section of part
nine. Biographees appear alphabetically with a list of references in which
information can be obtained. This section might be considered the first
index to Puerto Rican collective biography ever compiled. Only in recent
years have similar and more ambitious efforts been undertaken. [6]

Pedreira's desire was that his bibliography might serve as a starting
point for those who want to make new contributions to Puerto Rican culture.
It continues to be an excellent first step for any research on Puerto Rico and
has not been satisfactorily updated, in spite of several attempts, many of
which were published in local newspapers and journals but were not
exhaustive nor long-lived.

Augusto Bird, an economist at the University of Puerto Rico's Center
for Social Research, organized and contributed to the "Bibliografía
puertorriqueña de fuentes para investigaciones sociales: 1930-1945." This
work was published in 1947 in mimeograph as a preliminary edition.
Although it was meant to continue Pedreira's work, it emphasized the social
sciences and did not cover literary history. While Bird was responsible for
the economics section, Sol Luis Descartes contributed citations on social

sciences and Ramón Colón Torres provided references dealing with agriculture.

This provisional edition had many shortcomings, not the least of which were errors and inconsistencies in bibliographic information. The absence of a good index and a complete table of contents further limited the effectiveness of the work. The Center for Social Research continued to contribute bibliographies on recent publications in its annual reports. The efforts of María Stella O'Neill de López are especially meritorious. In 1977 the Center's **Bibliografía puertorriqueña de ciencias sociales** was finally published. Its two parts, organized by subject, cover from 1931 to 1954 and from 1954 to 1960. Regrettably, no indexes are included.

Meanwhile, Gonzalo Velázquez was compiling his **Anuario bibliográfico puertorriqueño**. The first volume corresponded to 1948. Velázquez deserves recognition for his dedication, enthusiasm and perseverance. In spite of many dificultes and delays in printing, Velázquez continued his important work through 1974. All types of publications are cited in one alphabet by author, title and subject. Complete bibliographic information appears under the title entry.

Velázquez also outlined a plan for bibliographic control of all materials published in or about Puerto Rico. His plan is worthy of careful examination by concerned scholars, librarians, writers and government officials responsible for preserving the cultural patrimony of the island. Recognizing the difficulties such a project would face, Velázquez suggested that the bibliography should consist of three parts: books, pamphlets, journals and newspapers; an index to journals; and an index to newspapers. Each part would be divided chronologically: works to 1930, works published from 1930 to 1950, and subdivisions by decades. The first step would be a revision of Pedreira's work. Velázquez stated that he had already prepared an exhaustive bibliography covering 1930 to 1950. However, this work has not been published and little has been done with regard to the other phases of the project he suggested.

Over the years different newspapers and journals have published bibliography sections in some issues. Among these are **El Mundo**, **Asomante**, **Revista del Instituto de Cultura Puertorriqueña**, **Caribbean Studies**, and **La Torre**. Unfortunately, these efforts usually have a very short life or are published irregularly. Bibliographies published in **Revista del Instituto de Cultura Puertorriqueña** and **Caribbean Studies** were revived recently after a lapse of several years.

Mainlanders have also shown great interest in compiling bibliographies on Puerto Rico, and on the experience of Puerto Ricans in the United States. As early as 1901, A. P. C. Griffin of the Library of Congress prepared **A List of Books on Porto Rico; with References to Periodicals**. It described resources owned by the Library, most of which had been acquired in 1898. Some brief contents notes are interspersed in this otherwise unannotated list. Other similar lists followed in later years.

In 1931 Harvard University sponsored Guillermo Rivera's **A Bibliography of the Belles-Lettres of Porto Rico**. It enjoyed a mixed reception. The most common criticism was the incompleteness of the work, since Rivera did not visit island collections during his research. Nevertheless, as Josefina Rivera de Alvarez admits, the Harvard list cited one work that was not found in Pedreira's bibliography. [8]

Probably the best-known bibliography originating in the continental United States is Paquita Vivó's **The Puerto Ricans**, published in 1973. It is a comprehensive, well-indexed, annotated work. Not surprisingly, its emphasis is on English-language sources.

More recently, important contributions have been made by Eleana Cevallos, the New York Public Library, Hunter College's Centro de Estudios Puertorriqueños, David Foster, Rosemary Brana-Shute, Diane Herrera and others. Many bibliographies on continental Puerto Ricans show a marked concern for educational and language issues. Return migration to Puerto Rico has also received more attention in the last decade. Angela and Ceferino Carrasquillo, Paquita Vivó, Nélida Pérez and Amílcar Tirado have all compiled excellent bibliographies on this topic. The years ahead should yield more works in this area.

In addition to general bibliographies on Puerto Rico or on Puerto Ricans on the mainland, a considerable number have been compiled on specific subjects. The most notable area is that of literature, although one might wish that more of the works had been annotated. The most valuable general source available is Josefina Rivera de Alvarez's **Diccionario de Literatura Puertorriqueña** which, in addition to biographical information, gives references to works by and about authors from all fields. A more recent publication, **Puerto Rican Literature: A Bibliography of Secondary Sources**, by David William Foster, is particularly useful for its references to criticisms of specific authors. While it does have some errors, it is one of the most comprehensive books available and may well motivate the preparation of similar works.

As for specific genres, in the field of drama Nilda González's **Bibliografía del teatro puertorriqueño** remains the standard, most complete bibliography yet published. One of the most important works on the Puerto Rican novel is the result of efforts by Edna Coll to prepare a bibliography on the Hispanic American novel and relevant critical works. Much remains to be done with regard to the short story. Lilian Quiles de la Luz edited her index in 1968, but little else has been done since that time.

Surprisingly, the genre in need of most attention is poetry. Puerto Rican literature has always been blessed with great poets and a reading audience with a great fondness for poetry. Unfortunately, the bibliographic record has not kept pace with poetic production. Cesáreo Rosa-Nieves prepared his **Indice bibliográfico para la poesía en Puerto Rico (1682-1942)** in 1943. Since that time, no comprehensive bibliography has been prepared. The Puerto Rican poetry journal **Mairena** does publish bibliographies on individual poets and occasionally on poetic movements. Lists of works published in 1979 and 1982 were published in the journal but these efforts have not been continued on an annual basis. Perhaps the poets most studied bibliographically have been Luis Palés Matos and Juan Antonio Corretjer.

Many authors have been the subject of bio-bibliographical lists. However, there is a real need for annotated works which would guide the researcher more efficiently and effectively. Important contemporary authors must surely be the object of future bibliographies: Edgardo Rodríguez Juliá, Rosario Ferré, Ana Lydia Vega, and others.   Similarly, attention should be given to prolific authors of earlier generations: Abelardo Díaz Alfaro, Manuel Méndez Ballester, Nilita Vientós, Francisco Arriví and many more. Other Puerto Rican patriots also await the dedication of interested bibliographers willing to spend the many months needed to prepare comprehensive, definitive, and annotated bibliographies on their lives and accomplishments.

History is another field that has received considerable attention from bibliographers. Investigators can rely on works by Pedreira, Mathews, Natal, Castro, Vila Vilar and others. Nonetheless, much remains to be done in regard to the historical and cultural record of the island's towns and cities. Only Bayamón, Ponce, Utuado and, to a lesser extent, Mayagüez, have been the subject of bibliographical compilations.   While Pedreira and Anderson include sections of basic sources on each municipality, these need to be supplemented by more comprehensive and up-to-date works.

Areas in which adequate bibliographies are still required include religion, philosophy, social problems and conditions, political science and many areas of science and technology. It is to be hoped that some interested persons will accept these challenges and compile the necessary works to fill these gaps.

Long ago in a tribute to Antonio S. Pedreira, Gustavo Agraít[9] stated that one of Don Antonio's greatest wishes was that someone would continue, on a yearly basis, the work he began in his **Bibliografía puertorriqueña**. Over a decade later it seemed that his wish might bear fruit when Gonzalo Velázquez began his **Anuario bibliográfico**. Regrettably, Velázquez was unable to issue it on a regular basis and 1974 saw the publication of the last volume. Since that time no serious attempt has been made at publishing a national bibliography. Although this situation is deplored periodically, no concrete action has been taken nor plans traced for solving the problem. It is incumbent upon concerned Puerto Ricans, government officials, and scholars to meet to determine a course of action and to obtain the necessary financial assistance to guarantee that an accurate, reliable and continuous record is kept of information written in and on Puerto Rico and Puerto Ricans who choose to move to the mainland. The longer the situation is ignored, the more difficult it will be to remedy. Moreover, without an adequate bibliographic record, present and future generations will have difficulty understanding their past in order to plan more realistically for their future.

NOTES

1. Later generations of the Géigel family continued to expand and care for the library. Several years ago this important collection was purchased by the University of Connecticut in Storrs.

2. Antonio S. Pedreira, "Los hallazgos del Sr. Géigel Sabat." In his **Aclaraciones y crítica** (Río Piedras, P.R.:   Editorial Phi Eta Mu, Universidad de Puerto Rico, 1941), p. 179.

3. Josefina Rivera de Alvarez, **Diccionario de Literatura Puertorriqueña**, 2d rev. ed.   (San Juan, P.R.:   Instituto de Cultura Puertorriqueña, 1970-1974), vol. 2, pt. 1: 681.

4. Francesco Cordasco, "Foreword." In **Bibliografía puertorriqueña, 1493-1930**, by Antonio S. Pedreira (New York: Burt Franklin Reprints, 1974), unpaged.

5. Antonio S. Pedreira, **Bibliografía puertorriqueña, 1493-1930** (Madrid: Imprenta de la Librería y Casa Editorial Hernando, 1932), p. xvii.

6. They are: Mundo Lo, Sara de. **Index to Spanish American Collective Biography**. Vol. 3: **The Central American and Caribbean Countries**. Boston: G. K. Hall, 1984, and Fowlie-Flores, Fay. **Index to Puerto Rican Collective Biography**. New York: Greenwood Press, 1987.

7. Gonzalo Velázquez, "La bibliografía en Puerto Rico." In **Seminario piloto de bibliografía: informe final** (La Habana, Cuba: Agrupación Bibliográfica Cubana José Toribio Medina, 1955), pp. 64-66.

8. Rivera de Alvarez, p.208.

9. Gustavo Agraít, "Tras recuerdos auténticos y uno apócrifo de Antonio S. Pedreira," **Ateneo Puertorriqueño** 3 (April, May, June 1939): 253.

Abbreviations

ACURIL	Association of Caribbean University and Research Libraries
CAAM	Colegio de Agricultura y Artes Mecánicas
ERIC	Educational Resources Information Center
KWIC	Key-word-in-context
n. s.	new series
P.R.	Puerto Rico
pt.	part
RUM	Recinto Universitario de Mayagüez
SALALM	Seminar on the Acquisition of Latin American Library Materials
U.P.R.	Universidad de Puerto Rico
U.S.	United States
vols.	volumes

Sources Consulted

Agrait, Gustavo. "Tras recuerdos auténticos y uno apócrifo de Antonio S. Pedreira." **Ateneo Puertorriqueño** 3 (April, May, June 1939): 250-54.

America: History and Life. Santa Barbara, Calif.: ABC-Clio, 1964-1967.

Bibliographic Index. New York: H.W. Wilson, 19 -

The Chicago Manual of Style. 13th ed. Chicago: University of Chicago Press, 1982.

Columbus Memorial Library. Pan American Union. **Index to Latin American Periodical Literature, 1929-1960.** 8 vols. Boston: G. K. Hall, 1962.

Cordeiro, Daniel Raposo. **A Bibliography of Latin American Bibliographies: Social Sciences and Humanities.** Metuchen, N.J.: Scarecrow Press, 1979.

_____. "Bibliography of Latin American Bibliographies." In **The Multifaceted Role of the Latin American Specialist,** edited by Seminar on the Acquisition of Latin American Library Materials (22nd: 1977: Gainesville, Fla.), 59-95. Austin, Tex.: SALALM Secretariat, 1979.

Drazan, Joseph Gerald. **An Annotated Bibliography of ERIC Bibliographies, 1966-1980.** Westport, Conn.: Greenwood Press, 1982.

Fowlie-Flores, Fay. **Index to Puerto Rican Collective Biography.** New York: Greenwood Press, 1987.

Gropp, Arthur E. **A Bibliography of Latin American Bibliographies**. Metuchen, N.J.: Scarecrow Press, 1968.

_____ **A Bibliography of Latin American Bibliographies. Supplement**. Metuchen, N.J.: Scarecrow Press, 1971.

_____ **A Bibliography of Latin American Bibliographies Published in Periodicals**. 2 vols. Metuchen, N.J.: Scarecrow Press, 1976.

HAPI: Hispanic American Periodicals Index. Los Angeles, Calif.: UCLA Latin American Center Publications, University of California, 1970-

Harner, James L. **On Compiling an Annotated Bibliography**. New York: Modern Language Association of America, 1985.

Historical Abstracts. Santa Barbara, Calif.: Clio Press, 1955-1987.

Indice general de publicaciones periódicas latinoamericanas: humanidades y ciencias sociales. Index to Latin American Periodicals: Humanities and Social Sciences.   vols. 1-10, no.2, 1961-April/June 1970. Boston: G. K. Hall, 1962-1971.

Laguerre, Enrique. "Don Antonio." **Isla** 2 (January 1940): 14-15.

Loroña, Lionel V. **Bibliography of Latin American Bibliographies, 1982-1983-** . Madison, Wis.: SALALM Secretariat, 1984-

Meléndez, Concha. "Antonio S. Pedreira: vida y expresión." **Ateneo Puertorriqueño** 3 (April, May, June 1939): 216-21.

Pedreira, Antonio S. "La bibliografía puertorriqueña de Harvard." In **Aclaraciones y crítica**, 19-31. Río Piedras, P.R.: Editorial Phi Eta Mu, Universidad de Puerto Rico, 1941.

_____ "Los hallazgos del Sr. Géigel Sabat." In **Aclaraciones y crítica,** 177-82. Río Piedras, P.R.: Editorial Phi Eta Mu, Universidad de Puerto Rico, 1941.

_____ "Listas de Coll y Toste y Paul G. Miller." **Ateneo Puertorriqueño** 3 (April, May, June 1939): 96-99.

Pérez de Rosa, Albertina. "Las bibliografías puertorriqueñas." **Boletín de la Sociedad de Bibliotecarios de Puerto Rico** 3 (January-April 1964): 7-17.

Piedracueva, Haydée. "Annual Report on Latin American and Caribbean Bibliographic Activity, 1980." In **Library Resources on Latin America: New Perspectives for the 1980s**, edited by Seminar on the Acquisition of Latin American Library Materials (25th: 1982: Washington, D.C.) 61-111. Madison, Wis.: SALALM Secretariat, 1981.

_____. "Bibliography of Bibliographies: 1982 Supplement." In **Public Policy Issues and Latin American Library Resources**, edited by Seminar on the Acquisition of Latin American Library Materials (27th: 1982: Washington, D.C.) 179-208. Los Angeles, Calif.: UCLA Latin American Center Publications, University of California, 1984.

_____. **A Bibliography of Latin American Bibliographies, 1975-1979: Social Sciences and Humanitites**. Metuchen, N.J.: Scarecrow Press, 1982.

Rivera de Alvarez, Josefina. **Diccionario de literatura puertorriqueña** 2d rev. ed. San Juan, P.R.: Instituto de Cultura Puertorriqueña, 1970-1974.

Rosario, Rubén del. "Al margen de la bibliografía." **Isla** 2 (January 1940): 2-3.

United States. Library of Congress. **Library of Congress Catalog. Books: Subjects**. Washington, D.C.: January-March, 1950-

Vázquez, Lourdes. "New Puerto Rican Bibliography." **SALALM Newsletter** 12 (June 1985): 3-4.

Velázquez, Gonzalo. **Anuario bibliográfico puertorriqueño: índice alfabético de libros, folletos, revistas y periódicos publicados en Puerto Rico...** Río Piedras, P.R.: Biblioteca de la Universidad, 1950-

_____. "La bibliografía en Puerto Rico." In **Seminario piloto de bibliografía: informe final**, edited by Seminario Bibliográfico de Centro América y el Caribe, 60-66. La Habana, Cuba: Agrupación Bibliográfica Cubana José Toribio Medina, 1955.

Zimmerman, Irene. **Current National Bibliographies of Latin America: A State of the Art Study**. Gainesville, Fla.: Center for Latin American Studies, University of Florida, 1971.

Zubatsky, David. "Annotated Bibliography of Latin American Author Bibliographies. Part II: Central America and the Caribbean." **Chasqui** 6

(1977): 41-72.

Annotated Bibliography of Puerto Rican Bibliographies

General Works

1.001. Albanell MacColl, Norah, et al. **Cuba, Dominican Republic, Haiti and Puerto Rico: A Selected Bibliography on the Caribbean Area Including Only Islands which Are Members of the Organization of American States.** Gainesville, Fla.: School of Inter-American Studies, University of Florida, 1956. 35 p.

> Covers materials published after 1950. Includes approximately 146 books, government documents and journal articles on Puerto Rico. No annotations or index.

1.002. Aponte de Otero, Pilar. "Bibliografía puertorriqueña; índice alfabético de libros, tesis y folletos relacionados con Puerto Rico: enero-octubre de 1970." **Boletín de la Sociedad de Bibliotecarios de Puerto Rico,** July-December 1970, pp. 75-78.

> A list of fifty-two books, theses and pamphlets written about Puerto Rico or published in Puerto Rico during the first ten months of 1970.

1.003. Aponte de Otero, Pilar. "Bibliografía puertorriqueña." **Boletín de la Sociedad de Bibliotecarios de Puerto Rico,** January-June 1973, pp. 125-31.

> A continuation of the previous entry (1.002).

1.004. Association of Caribbean University and Research Libraries. Comité Central de Bibliografía. "Bibliografía de bibliografías del Caribe (versión preliminar); sometida a la VII Conferencia de la Asociación de Bibliotecas Universitarias y de Investigación del Caribe, Willemstad, Curazao, 21-26 de septiembre de 1975." San Juan, P.R.: Secretaría General de la Asociación de Bibliotecas Universitarias y de Investigación del Caribe, 1975. 209 p. (mimeographed)

This useful bibliography of bibliographies compiled in or on Caribbean countries has never been published. The section on Puerto Rico can be found on pages 150 to 158 and includes about seventy-two entries, many on general topics with no particular emphasis on Puerto Rico.

1.005.   Ateneo Puertorriqueño. **Catálogo por orden alfabético de autores y de materias de las obras existentes en la Biblioteca del Ateneo Puertorriqueño.** [San Juan, P.R.:] Tipografía "El País", 1897. 63 p.

A list of materials owned by the Puerto Rican Atheneum. For each title the following information is given : author, title and number of volumes or format. For some items, the exact physical location was also noted. There is a section of works by various authors in collaboration which includes journals. A great many of the items described were written by Puerto Ricans or about Puerto Ricans.

1.006.   Baa, Enid M., comp. **Doctoral Dissertations and Selected Theses on Caribbean Topics Accepted [sic] by Universities of Canada, United States and Europe, from 1778-1968.** St. Thomas, Virgin Islands: Bureau of Public Libraries & Museums, Dept. of Conservation & Cultural Affairs, Government of the Virgin Islands of the U.S., 1969. 91 p.

This computer-produced bibliography consists of two parts: doctoral dissertations (1-1010) and selected masters theses (1011-1247). Includes indexes by key word in context, author, year and university. Titles related to Puerto Rico can be identified by consulting the KWIC index.

1.007.   Baa, Enid M., comp. **Theses on Caribbean Topics, 1778-1968.** San Juan, P.R.: Institute of Caribbean Studies & University of Puerto Rico Press, 1970. 146 p. (Caribbean Bibliographic Series, no.1)

Similar to the previous title, this publication describes five fewer doctoral dissertations. The indexes are by university, countries studied, subject and year of presentation.

1.008.   "Background Books: Puerto Rico." **Wilson Quarterly** 4 (Spring 1980): 150-53.

"This essay is based on research conducted by Barbara Mauger, an intern at the Wilson Center's Latin American Program. Former U.S. Ambassador to Bolivia Ben Stephansky, Wilson Center Fellow Angel A. Rama, and Jorge Heine also advised on the selection of titles." The references cited are in English and include general books about Puerto Rico.

1.009.   Bayitch, S.A.   Latin America and the Caribbean: A **Bibliographical Guide to Works in English.**   Coral Gables, Fla.: University of Miami Press, 1967. 943 p. (University of Miami School of Law. Interamerican Legal Studies, 10)

> The main divisions of this work are by country or geographic region. Each of these is further subdivided by topic. Only English-language books and journal articles are cited. A section of general bibliographies is also included. Author, subject and area indexes assure the usefulness of this publication. References to Puerto Rico appear on pages 901 to 923.

1.010.   Becco, Horacio Jorge. **Contribución para una bibliografía de las ideas latinoamericanas.** Paris: Unesco, 1981. 230 p.

> No annotations accompany the entries which are grouped into major divisions: general bibliography; essays on Latin America; and regional studies. The Puerto Rican section of about fifty-eight entries appears to be a list of general references. The most recent work cited was published in 1975. Name index.

1.011.   Berlin. Ibero-Amerikanisches Institut. **Schlagwortkatalog des Ibero-Amerikanischen Institut: Preussischer Kulturbesitz in Berlin. Subject Catalog of the Iber-American Institute: Prussian Cultural Heritage Foundation in Berlin.** 30 vols. Boston: G.K. Hall, 1977.

> This is the printed catalog of the largest European institution which collects Latin American and Iberean materials in all disciplines. Unlike many such catalogs, it includes journal articles as well as books and monogragphs. There are different sets of volumes for general subjects, countries, other place names, and personal names. Includes a bilingual (German-English) list of headings. The collection is strongest in the areas of archeology and ethnology.

1.012.   Betancourt, J. A.   "Articles on Puerto Rico from **La Torre; Revista de la Universidad de Puerto Rico.**" New York: Library, Centro de Estudios Puertorriqueños, City University of New York, 1973.   3 p. (mimeographed)

> Identifies articles on Puerto Rico published in **La Torre,** one of the University of Puerto Rico's oldest and most distinguished journals.

This listing covers materials published from 1953 to 1961 and is arranged alphabetically in two parts: history-social sciences and literature.

1.013.   **Bibliografía de Centroamérica y del Caribe.** Compiled under the auspices of Unesco by the Agrupación Bibliográfica Cubana José Toribio Medina . Technical director: Fermín Peraza Sarausa. La Habana, Cuba; Madrid: La Agrupación, 1956-1960.

> Publisher varies. This annual publication lasted only a few years. It was an annotated listing of both governmental and private publications of the countries of the region. Most, if not all, the information on Puerto Rican materials was contributed by Gonzalo Velázquez. Arranged by subject and supplemented by an author index.

1.014.   "Bibliografía puertorriqueña." **Revista del Instituto de Cultura Puertorriqueña** 43 (April-June 1969)-

> Briefly commentated bibliography of books, magazines and pamphlets published in Puerto Rico in a given year. It was issued in different numbers, usually in the last one of each year from 1969 to 1971. Publication resumed with number 90, October-December of 1985. Most compilations are attributed to Juan Martínez Picó, a distinguished Puerto Rican critic.

1.015.   **Bibliographic Guide to Latin American Studies**, 1978-Boston: G. K. Hall, 1979-

> Issued annually in multivolume sets. A dictionary catalog of works which can be found in the University of Texas's Nettie Lee Benson Latin American Collection. This is a supplement to the University of Texas at Austin's **Catalog of the Latin American Collection**, published by G. K. Hall, with a sixteen volume supplement published from 1971 to 1975. Includes full bibliographic information on all materials catalogued in the Latin American Collection, as well as some books in the Library of Congress. Entries are by author, title and subject in one alphabet. Works dealing with Puerto Rico can be found under "Puerto Rico", "Puerto Rican..." and names of specific persons or places.

1.016.   **Bibliographic Index**. New York: H. W. Wilson, 1938-

> This important index cites bibliographies included in books, theses, and journal articles, including general and special topic bibliographies. Also covers separately published bibliographies.

1.017.   Bird, Augusto. "Bibliografía puertorriqueña de fuentes para investigaciones sociales, 1946-1947. Provisional ed. 2 vols. Río Piedras, P.R.: Centro de Investigaciones Sociales, Universidad de Puerto Rico, 1946-1947. (mimeographed)

> Attempts to update Pedreira's **Bibliografía puertorriqueña** (1.090) althouh it does not include literary history. This unannotated listing is arranged in eight sections, each of which is subdivided by topics: bibliographical sources; general information; natural history; health; economy; political and administrative history; cultural organization; and Puerto Rican history. Optimum use of this work is impeded by the lack of indexes. There are also some inconsistencies in style.

1.018.   "Books on Puerto Rico." **Library Journal**, 15 March 1956, pp. 672-73.

> This short list of forty-five English-language sources found in the New York Public Library gives authors and titles only. It is taken from the **Branch Library Book News** of the New York Public Library for February of 1956.

1.019.   **Borinquen: lista bilingüe de libros, películas y discos sobre la experiencia puertorriqueña; A Bilingual List of Books, Films and Records on the Puerto Rican Experience.** New York: La Biblioteca Pública de Nueva York, El Sistema de Sucursales, La Oficina de Servicios para Adultos; The New York Public Library, The Branch Library System, The Office of Adult Services, 1974. 32 p.

> This "third edition of a bibliography originally published in 1963 under the title **Puerto Rico**" is a bilingual, annotated listing of some 163 items. Includes an author-title index. Although the emphasis is on Puerto Rico, it does include many references to the mainland experience. It is organized under the following topics: general works; history; social sciences; literature (by genre);language; the arts; biography; films; and records.

1.020.   Bourne, Dorothy Dulles. **Bibliography**. 1966 10 p. (ED 019 333)
> This is a partially annotated list of books and articles on socio-economic changes in Puerto Rico from 1931 to 1962.

1.021.   Bravo, Enrique. **Bibliografía puertorriqueña selecta y anotada.** Translated by Marcial Cuevas. New York: The Urban Center, Columbia University [1972] 115, 114 p.

A selective, bilingual bibliography of titles considered to be
"classics" and the most relevant to the Puerto Rican experience.
Newspaper and journal articles as well as unpublished theses are
excluded. Chapters cover anthropology and sociology, political
science, cultural development, economy, education, geography,
history, linguistics, literature, Puerto Rico and the Hispanic world,
religion and philosophy, magazines, reference works, bibliographies
and official publications. At the end of each chapter can be found a
supplementary bibliography. An appendix and a general index are
included as well.

1.022.   Brooklyn College.   Institute of Puerto Rican Studies.   **The
Puerto Rican People: A Selected Bibliography for Use in Social
Work Education.** New York: Council on Social Work Education, 1973. 54 p.

Divided into two sections, one on Puerto Rico and one on Puerto
Ricans in the United States, this bibliography uses different symbols
to indicate the topics discussed in each item. Emphasizes social
change and social problems but also includes materials which describe Puerto Rican society in general from an historic or contemporary point of view.

1.023.   Brown, Doris R. **Puerto Rico: A Checklist of Materials in
the University of Connecticut Library.** With Joanne Akeroyd, Charity
Chang, and Mohini Mundkur. Storrs, Conn.: The University of Connecticut
Library, 1976. 81 p.

A selective listing of over 700 items owned by the University Library
as of January of 1979. Items are arranged by title under seven
categories and a journal section. Author index. The bibliography does
not cover an important private collection of Puerto Rican materials
which was purchased from the Geigel family posterior to the compilation of the work.

1.024.   Brown, Lyle C. **Latin America: A Bibliography.** Kingsville,
Tex.: Texas College of Arts and Industries, 1962. 79 p.

Pages 56 to 59 list materials on Puerto Rico written in English.
Although somewhat dated, this source is a frequently-cited one.

1.025.   Capelis, Crystal and Linda M. Bretz. "Spanish-Language Books
for Children of Puerto Rican Heritage." **Booklist** 72 (February 1976): 793-
94.

Briefly annotated bibliography of "books chosen specifically for their expression of Puerto Rican themes and culture." The grade level is indicated for each of the twenty-seven items described.

1.026.   "Caribeña;   bibliografía   actual/Current   Bibliography."
Caribbean Studies 20 (1988)-

After a lapse of eight years, the journal **Caribbean Studies** has resumed publication. "Caribeña", formerly entitled "Current Bibliography", is a regular section which cites recent books, pamphlets and articles. It is arranged by area and country and includes a section on Puerto Rico. All fields of interest are covered, except the natural sciences. Neida Pagán Jiménez is responsible for the latest compilations.

1.027.   Carreras de Santiago, Jennie. **Inventario general de la Biblioteca del Centro de Investigaciones Sociales-U.P.R.-a dic. 1974.** Río Piedras, P.R.: 1974? various pagings

Following brief histories of the library and the Center, the author includes a bibliography of the library's books arranged by author, a list of journals with holdings, a bibliography of investigations, articles and monographs produced by the Center or its members (arranged alphabetically under books, monographs, articles, and pamphlets), a list of materials in the folklore collection on differect countries including Puerto Rico, a list of government publications by department or agency and a list of United Nations publications held by the library. The lackof a subject index tends to limit the usefulness of this work.

1.028.   **Catalog of the Cuban and Caribbean Library, University of Miami, Coral Gables, Florida.** 6 vols. Boston: G. K. Hall, 1977.

Volume five of this large library's card catalog has entries under Puerto Rico" and "Puerto Rican..." A useful location tool.

1.029.   **Catálogo del establecimiento de José J. Acosta.** Puerto Rico: 1882. 38 p.

Entries which give author, title and price, are grouped under these headings: medicine; religious works; other works; and works of primary instruction. The list is not in strict alphabetical order. It includes works by Acosta y Calvo.

1.030.   **Catálogo general de la Librería Real Hermanos**. San Juan,
P.R.: Real Hermanos Tip., 1921. 64 p.

> A catalog of books available at the Real Hermanos Bookstore in
> 1921. While most of the books were of general interest, many titles
> were written by/about Puerto Ricans. Only author, title and price
> were given. Of historical interest.

1.031.   Cevallos, Eleana E., comp. **Puerto Rico**. Edited by Sheila R.
Herstein.   Oxford, Eng.; Santa Barbara, Calif.:   Clio Press, 1985.   193 p.
(World Bibliographical Series, 52)

> Books and journal articles published since 1970 are annotated in this
> selective bibliography. Items published before 1970 but considered to
> be classics or which deal with subjects about which little else has
> been written are also cited. This work is meant to serve the general
> reader, not the specialist. Mainly English-language sources are re-
> ferred to in this subject-arranged compilation. An excellent general
> index adds to the book's usefulness.

1.032.   Colegio Regional de Cayey.   Biblioteca.   **Las publicaciones
oficiales del gobierno del Estado Libre Asociado de Puerto Rico;
bibliografía**. Cayey, P.R.: 1968. 75 p.

> This is the only existing bibliography of government publications and
> was originally prepared for a SALALM meeting in 1969. It is organ-
> ized by government agencies. The information given varies accord-
> ing to the agency that submitted the information. Ana Margarita
> Ramírez de Alemañy was the library director at the time this unique
> work was prepared.

1.033.   Coll y Toste, Cayetano. "Bibliografía puertorriqueña." **Puerto
Rico Ilustrado**, numbers 19-28, 1910.

> This was a short-lived attempt to publish a Puerto Rican bibliography
> in one of the most prestigious magazines of the period. It was retro-
> spective as well as current and cited journals, periodicals and books.
> Short descriptions of the content of each item were given. It only
> covered the letter A, reaching the author Asenjo. Nevertheless, it
> was an authoritative attempt. Coll y Toste was a highly respected
> historian.

1.034.   Conference on Inter-Library Cooperation and Exchange (1969:
San Juan, P.R.) **Official Records**. San Juan, P.R.: Commonwealth of Puerto

Rico, Caribbean Economic Development Corporation (CODECA), 1969. 1 vol. (Document no. 071/1/69E)

> Included in the proceedings is a "List of Puerto Rican Periodicals and Newspapers at the Puerto Rican Collection UPR Library." Unfortunately, holdings are not indicated. The conference was sponsored by the U.S. Virgin Islands Department of Conservation and Cultural Affairs, Division of Libraries and Museums and CODECA.

1.035.   Council on Interracial Books for Children. "100 Children's Books about Puerto Ricans: A Study in Racism, Sexism and Colonialism. **Interracial Books for Children** 4 (1972): 1-16.

> No copy was obtained of this article cited by Cotera (2.349, p.87).

1.036.   Cundall, Frank.   **Bibliography of the West Indies (Excluding Jamaica**. Kingston, Jamaica: The Institute of Jamaica, 1909. 179 p.

> A short section of books and pamphlets relating to Puerto Rico can be found on pages 18 and 19. This work is cited frequently.

1.037.   **Current Caribbean Bibliography. Bibliografía actual del Caribe**. Hato Rey, P.R.: Caribbean Regional Library, 1951-1973.

> Frequency, arrangement, publisher and title varied for this bibliography of publications of the Caribbean countries. When the arrangement was by format, then by country, references to Puerto Rican materials appeared in each of these sections: periodicals and newspapers; government serials; and monographs. A list of publishers and addresses is to be found in each issue. Some cumulations were published.

1.038.   Deal, Carl W., ed. **Latin America and the Caribbean: A Dissertation Bibliography**. Ann Arbor, Mich.:   University Microfilms International [1977] 164 p.

> Arranged by subject, then geographically by country studied, this bibliography lists 7,200 dissertations published by University Microfilms International through 1977. It supersedes the company's **Latin America: A Catalog of Dissertations**, published in 1974. Each entry includes author, dissertation title, degree granted, year, university, number of pages, a reference to the appropriate listing in **Dissertation Abstracts International**, and a publication number. Entries for Puerto Rico can be found under all subjects except

chemistry, fine arts and library and information science. Author
index appended. This work is updated by **Latin America and the
Caribbean II: A Dissertation Bibliography** published in 1980
(1.064).

1.039.   **Dokumentationsdienst   Lateinamerika/Documentación
latinoamérica;   ausgewaehlte   neuere   Literatur/boletín
bibliográfico.**   Hamburg: Deutsches   Uebersee-Institut,   Uebersee-
Dokumentation-Referat Lateinamerika, 1971-

> Published four times a year, this bibliography of journal articles is
> organized by country, then by subject. Information on libraries having
> copies of the items is included. References to articles relating
> to Puerto Rico, mainly in English and Spanish, can be found by
> consulting the geographic index.

1.040.   Dossick, Jesse J. **Doctoral Research on Puerto Rico and
Puerto Ricans**. New York: School of Education, New York University, 1967.
34 p.

> A bibliography of 320 doctoral dissertations presented at mainland
> universities but dealing with Puerto Rico and Puerto Ricans. More
> than half were accepted since 1950. Arranged by discipline, the list
> covers the arts, sciences and education. No annotations are given.
> Author index. (Also reprinted in **The Puerto Ricans: Migration
> and General Bibliography**. New York: Arno Press, 1975)

1.041.   **Fichero Bibligráfico Hispanoamericano**. San Juan, P.R.:
Melcher Ediciones, 1961-

> Publisher varies. Eleven issues are published yearly to provide in-
> formation on new books published in Spanish. All Spanish American
> countries, including Puerto Rico, are covered. Organized roughly
> by Dewey Decimal numbers, each issue has indexes by title and
> author. Prices are given when available. A list of publishers and
> dealers is appended.

1.042.   Franklin D. Roosevelt Library, Hyde Park, New York. "Papers of
Rexford G. Tugwell, 1911-1972."   Hyde Park, N.Y.:   General Services
Administration, National Archives and Records Service, Franklin D.
Roosevelt Library, 1977. 39 p. (mimeographed)

> Tugwell served as governor of Puerto Rico from 1941 to 1946. This
> inventory of his papers is organized by container, with a brief des-

cription of their contents. Many references can be found to information and documents on Puerto Rico, especially in containers twenty-
six to thirty.

1.043.   Gautier de Villafañe, Aida.   **Lista de libros Colección
Puertorriqueña Sala Manuel María Sama**. Mayagüez, P.R.:   C.A.A.M.,
1977. 176 p.

Alphabetical list of books found in the Puerto Rican Collection of the
Library of the University of Puerto Rico, Mayagüez Campus. This
campus is the seconu iargest on the island. A supplement would
increase the usefulness and currentness of this publication.

1.044.   Géigel Polanco, Vicente.   "Bibliografía   puertorriqueña."
Asomante 2 (January-March 1946): 77-81.

A list of eighty books and pamphlets published during 1945. Unfortunately this listing was not continued in the following years.

1.045.   Géigel y Zenón, José and Abelardo Morales Ferrer. **Bibliografía
puertorriqueña**. First edition published by Fernando J. Géigel y Sabat.
Barcelona, Spain: Editorial Araluce, 1934. 462 p.

This important pioneering work was based on the personal library of
the principal author, José Géigel y Zenón. Approximately 498 entries
make up the main body of the book which was submitted to the 1893
exhibition celebrated to commemorate the discovery of Puerto Rico.
Although incomplete, the bibliography won a gold medal. Fernando J.
Géigel Sabat later prepared four useful indexes for the first published
edition: author; title; chronological; and subject. Covering to 1894,
this annotated compilation is organized alphabetically in three
sections: books written and printed in Puerto Rico from 1807 when,
the author asserts, the first printing press was brought into the
country; books written in Puerto Rico or elsewhere, by Puerto Ricans,
and printed in Spain or other countries; books written by other
nationals and printed outside Puerto Rico but dealing with some
aspect of the island. Many of the annotations make critical
commentaries. An appendix provides additional information about
sources cited in the book.

1.046.   Gladden, Earle M. "Puerto Rican Books." **Booklist** 70 (March 15,
1974):   775-79; 72 (February 1, 1976):   757-58; 73 (March 15, 1977):
1079-80; 75 (October 15, 1978): 365-66.

Title varies: October 15, 1978 issue entitled "Puerto Rican Books in Spanish." Brief annotations describe books written in Spanish by Puerto Rican authors or about Puerto Rico and Puerto Ricans.

1.047.   Grieb, Kenneth J., ed. **Research Guide to Central America and the Caribbean**. Madison, Wis.: The University of Wisconsin Press, 1985. 431 p.

Contains descriptions of major archival depositories or research centers, and bibliographic essays which also suggest areas for further research. The main section on Puerto Rico was written by Blanca G. Silvestrini and María de los Angeles Castro. Their article appears to be the same as the one published in **Latin American Research Review** (2.154).

1.048.   Hadgis, Diana. **Puerto Rican Heritage: An Annotated Bibliography of the Puerto Rican Experience**. New York: BCC (Bronx Community College), 1979. 26p (BCC Library Heritage Series)

Brief annotations describe 146 books found in the Bronx Community Library. Citations are grouped by broad subject categories: land and culture; society; history; education; literature; biography; and blibliography. Covers both Spanish and English titles on Puerto Rico and on Puerto Ricans in the United States.

1.049.   **Handbook   of   Latin   American   Studies**.   Vol.   1–Gainesville, Fla.: University of Florida Press, 1935–

Perhaps the most important general bibliography for Latin American studies. This annual publication often features special topic and/or geographic bibliographies, including some for Puerto Rico. Beginning with volume twenty-six, it was divided into two parts: humanities and social sciences. Each is published in alternate years.

1.050.   Heine, Jorge. "Puerto Rico, 1952–1982: A Bibliographic Guide." In **Time for Decision: The United States and Puerto Rico**, edited by Jorge Heine, 277–300. Lanham, Md.: North-South Publishing Co., 1983.
A "selective, thematic guide to the literature on Puerto Rico, Puerto Ricans, and U.S.-Puerto Rican relations since...1952 and continuing on to 1982..." Approximately 248 Spanish and English titles are cited on the following topics: government; the party system; Muñoz Marín; ideology and public opinion; trade unions and politics; economy; society and culture; migration and the diaspora; U.S.-Puerto Rican relations and Puerto Rico; and the international system. A very useful contribution.

1.051.   Henández Ramos, Josefina.   "Desglose [bibliográfico de la revista] **Puerto Rico Ilustrado**, 1931-1935." Master's thesis, University of Puerto Rico, 1972.

   For many years **Puerto Rico Ilustrado** was one of the island's most important magazines. This index of the years mentioned is arranged chronologically. Entries refer to the issue number, article title, genre if applicable, author, and page. The name index refers to entries by and about each person. The "subject index" is not very useful because it covers general topics only and is **not** arranged alphabetically. See Colón Jiménez (2.005) for an index to the same magazine for the years 1910 to 1920.

1.052.   Hill, Marnesba D.   "Bibliography of Puerto Rican History and Literature."   New York: Herbert H. Lehman College Library, 1972.   31 p. (mimeographed)

   This is a list of materials found in the Herbert H. Lehman College Library. Arranged in five sections: reference books, biography; education; history and social science; language, literature; and the arts. A short list of relevant periodicals is appended. In December of 1974 a twenty-seven-page supplement was issued. Some typographical errors and mistakes in proper names will be encountered .

1.053.   Hispanic Society of America. **Catalogue of the Library**.   10 vols. Boston: G. K. Hall, 1962. **Supplement**. 4 vols. 1970.

   Most specific references to Puerto Rico and Puerto Ricans can be found in volume eight of the original publication.

1.054.   Hostos, Adolfo de. **Tesauro de datos históricos**. 3 vols. San Juan, P.R.: Departamento de Hacienda, 1948-1951.

   Only three volumes of this monumental work by Puerto Rico's Official Historian have ever been published in book form. The remainder of this important compendium can be found on the original index cards kept in the Library at the University of Puerto Rico's Center for Historical Research (Centro de Investigaciones Históricas). Since it indexes a great many books, reports, journals, newspapers and other materials, it constitutes a good bibliographical starting point for general and historical information about Puerto Rico and its towns. The published version includes a complete bibliography of sources consulted.

1.055.   Hurwitz, Edith F. "Caribbean Studies, Part II: Puerto Rico."
Choice 12 (December 1975): 1271-72+

The following topics are touched upon in this bibliographic essay:
bibliography and reference books; general background; history and
political science; economics and business; sociology, anthropology,
education; and Puerto Ricans in the United States. Complete
bibliographical information is supplied in the "Works Cited" section.

1.056.   Indiana University Libraries. **Pueblo Latino**. Vol. 2: **The
Puerto Ricans**. Bloomington, Ind.: Indiana University, 1975. 107 p.

This unannotated bibliography of materials owned by the library is
divided into the following sections: bibliographies and other resources; Puerto Rican history; humanities and publications of general
interest; social sciences; government publications and documents.
Approximately 1200 Spanish and English-language sources are cited.
No index.

1.057.   Instituto de Cultura Puertorriqueña. **Proyecto para un
programa de publicaciones: serie biblioteca puertorriqueña**. San
Juan, P.R.: 195? 108 p.

A prospectus for an important project of the Institute of Puerto Rican
Culture in which annotated editions of the cardinal works of the
island's literary and intellectual heritage would be published. As
such, it constitutes a useful general bibliography. Citations appear
under the following headings: complete works; chroniclers,
historians, memoirs and historical sources (folklores); novels,
stories, drama, "zarzuelas"; journalists, poets and essayists; art,
biography, bibliography; sciences and scientific dissemination; guides
to Puerto Rico; and voyagers. Bibliographical information varies
greatly from complete detail to author and title only. Some
explanatory notes are included.

1.058.   Inter-American Book Exchange, Washington, D.C. **Index to
Latin American Books, 1938-**   Washington, D.C.: 1940-

A bibliography of "all the information available regarding the printed
output, except periodicals, of...Latin America and Puerto Rico."
References appear under author and subject headings in Spanish.
Materials relating to Puerto Rico can be found by author, specific
subject and under the heading "Puerto Rico."

1.059.   Jones, C. K.   **A Bibligraphy of Latin American Bibliographies.** 2d ed. Washington, D.C.:   United States Government Printing Office, 1942. 311 p.

> Arranged by country with one "general and miscellaneous" section. Entries for Puerto Rico can be found on pages 256 to 258. General index. Rather dated but frequently cited.

1.060.   Kidder, Frederick E. and Allen David Bushong. "Bibliography of Doctoral Dissertations Relating to Puerto Rico Accepted by United States Colleges and Universities through 1955-56."   **Southeastern Latin Americanist** 2 (September 1958): 5-12.

> For each of 127 dissertations the following details are given: author, title, university and year of presentation. A supplement which appeared in the December 1958 issue of the same magazine included twenty-two additional works for 1956-1957.

1.061.   _____ "Periodicals Published in Puerto Rico." In **Final Report and Working Papers,** edited by Seminar on the Acquisition of Latin American Library Materials, (5th: 1960), 289-93. Washington, D.C.: Pan American Union, 1955.

> Kidder was a well-known political scientist and librarian. His list of 31 periodicals provides the following data for each: journal title, frequency, publisher and cost. The first publication date is not indicated. Some brief annotations are given.

1.062.   _____ "Puerto Rico al día: A Brief Bibliography." **Doors to Latin America** (Gainesville, Fla.) 3 (October 1956): 12.

> True to its subtitle, this brief listing includes only about twenty-eight sources on Puerto Rico.

1.063.   _____ and Allen David Bushong, comp. **Theses on Pan American Topics Prepared by Candidates for Doctoral Degrees in Universities and Colleges in the United States and Canada.** 4th ed. Washington, D.C.:   Pan American Union, General Secretariat of the Organization of American States, 1962. 124 p. (Columbus Memorial Library. Bibliographic Series, 5, 4th ed.)

> This list covers doctoral dissertations only and is arranged alphabetically by author. Dissertation title, institution and year are also indicated. Indexes are by istitution and subject, allowing for the identification of studies dealing with the island.

1.064.   **Latin America and the Caribbean II: A Dissertation Bibliography.** Edited by Marian C. Walters. Ann Arbor, Mich.: University Microfilms International, 1980. 78 p.

> "This compilation of 1,868 doctoral dissertations and 100 masters theses is an update to **Latin America and the Caribbean: A Dissertation Bibliography** edited by Carl W. Deal..." (1.038). As is the case of the earlier work, this bibliography is arranged by subject and subdivided by country or area. An added feature is that in many cases the United States has been further subdivided by ethnic groups, including USA-Puerto Ricans. In this supplement, referencesto Puerto Rico and/or Puerto Ricans in the United States can be found under all subjects except business administration, chemistry, fine arts, health sciences, mass communications, mathematics and statistics, philosophy and speech. Author index included.

1.065.   Ledesma, Moisés. **Bibliografía cultural de Puerto Rico (anotada).** San Juan, P.R.: Plus Ultra Educational Publishers, Inc., 1970. 103 p.

> A partially annotated bibliography of poetry, music, theater and painting in Puerto Rico, arranged alphabetically under each genre. In many instances, only author and title are provided. The absence of a general index tends to limit even further the use of this work.

1.066.   **Listín: exclusivamente libros de Puerto Rico.**   Río Piedras, P.R.: Familia Freixas, 1947. 34 p.

> Cover title: **Listín número tres de libros de P.R. que ofrece a la venta La Villa del Libro.** The first list was published in 1945 and a second in 1946. This is a price list arranged by title. Initial articles are used in alphabetizing. Largely of historical interest.

1.067.   López, Adalberto. "Puerto Ricans and the Literature of Puerto Rico." **Journal of Ethnic Studies** 1 (1973): 56-65.

> "A bibliographical essay on the history, social and political literature of Puerto Rico and the Puerto Rican community in the United States." The author asserts that until recently Puerto Rican studies were scarce and their quality usually discouraging. Following the expansion of black studies, the literature on Puerto Ricans both on the mainland and on the island improved in coverage and depth. Critical commentaries are made on the works cited.

1.068.   López, Adalberto. "Some of the Literature on Puerto Rico and
Puerto Ricans in English."   In **Puerto Rico and the Puerto Ricans:
Studies in History and Society,** edited by Adalberto López and James
Petras, 471-80. New York: John Wiley, 1974.

This bibliographichal essay evaluates literature about Puerto Rico and
its people, published from the 1960s to 1974.

1.069.   López, Daniel. "A Critique of Bibliographies on Puerto Rico and
Puerto Ricans."   **Newsletter** (National Association of Interdisciplinary
Studies for Native American, Black, Chicano, Puerto Rican and Asian
Americans) 1 (December 1975): 7-12.

This general criticism of contemporary Puerto Rican bibliographies
asserts that most "are filled with sources which, in effect support
the colonial regime." The author focuses on Adalberto López's essays
to illustrate the general shortcomings of contemporary bibliographical studies, according to his point of view.

1.070.   López de Díaz, Aura A. **El periodismo en Puerto Rico: una
bibliografía de libros, artículos de periódicos, artículos de
revistas y otros materiales relacionados.** 2 vols. Río Piedras, P.R.:
Escuela de Comunicación Pública, Universidad de Puerto Rico, 1978.

The first volume is arranged alphabetically under three subjects:
journalism in general; Puerto Rican newspapers; and Puerto Rican
journalists. The second volume covers associations of journalists,
laws and legislation, and the study and teaching of journalism.

1.071.   Loroña, Lionel V.   **Bibliography of Latin American
Bibliographies, 1982-1983-** . Madison, Wis.: Secretariat, Seminar on
the Acquisition of Latin American Library Materials, Memorial Library,
University of Wisconsin, Madison, 1984-

"This publication replaces the **Anual Report on Latin American
and Caribbean Bibliographic Activities,** which used to be
published as a working paper in the **Papers** (earlier, **Final Report
and Working Papers**) of the annual seminar." It is meant to supplement Arthur Gropp's work (see "Sources Consulted"). It is organized
by broad subjects and has author and subject indexes. To locate
bibliographies related to Puerto Rico, consult the subject index under
"Puerto Rican" and "Puerto Rico" and/or the specific subject with
Puerto Rico as a subdivision. For bibliographies on individual Puerto
Ricans, consult the subject index or the section "Personal bibliogra-

phies" or "Biography (Individual)". Coverage does not include bibliographies appened to books or chapters of books, or to journal articles. The title of this important source varies slightly.

1.072.   Martínez Capó, Juan.   "Las pequeñas revistas literarias (Panorama: 1930-1954)." **Asomante** 11 (January-March 1955): 102-123.

Small magazines published between 1930 and 1954 are described in this bibliographic essay. Publication data and a brief history are given for each title. Martínez, a distinguished literary critic, also analyzes the magazine's content and names important contributors to each.

1.073.   Mathews, Thomas.   "Documentación sobre Puerto Rico en la Biblioteca del Congreso." **Historia** 6 (October 1956): 89-140.

An important bibliographic essay on Puerto Rican materials found in the Library of Congress during the summer of 1956. The appendices list and/or describe the materials studied: Appendix A: Reproductions of Manuscripts in the British Museum; Appendix B: Reproductions of Manuscripts in the French National Library; Appendix C: Reproductions of Manuscripts in El Archivo General de Indias; Appendix D: General Puerto Rican Holdings of the Manuscripts Division; Appendix E: Puerto Rican Memorial Collection (**Informe de Dr. Morales Carrión**); Appendix F: A Catalogue of the Manuscripts Contained in the Alice B. Gould Purchase Now Known as the Puerto Rican Memorial Collection and Found in the Manuscripts Division of the Library of Congress; Appendix G: Material in the Rare Books Division; Appendix H: Material in the Newspaper Collection; Appendix I: The Division of Maps of the Library of Congress; Appendix J: Prints,Photographs; and Appendix K: The Law Library of the Library of Congress. The latter includes a selective list ofpamphlets in the Alice B. Gould collection. Mathews signals those titles not mentioned in Pedreira's bibliography. Some sections of the bibliography should be revised as to status or location.

1.074.   Matos, Antonio. **Guía a las reseñas de libros de y sobre Hispanoamérica. A Guide to Reviews of Books from and about Hispanic America.** Río Piedras, P.R.: 1973; Detroit: Blaine Ethridge, 1976-

A bibliographic guide compiled by an experienced, highly-respected Puerto Rican librarian. Meant to be an annual publication, it is very slow, the latest volume being that for 1984. Includes bibliogrphical references to and short summaries of books published by/about

Puerto Ricans as well as citations to journal and newspaper reviews of those works. Arranged alphabetically, the guide is well indexed.

1.075.   Medina, José Toribio. **La imprenta en algunas ciudades de la América Española, 1754-1823**. Amsterdam, The Netherlands: N. Israel, 1964. 116 p.

Original title: **Notas bibliográficas referentes a las primeras producciones de la imprenta en algunas ciudades de la América española**. Describes, in chronological order, eight of the first books published in Puerto Rico.

1.076.   Miller, E. Willard and Ruby M. Miller. **Middle America and the Caribbean: A Bibliography on the Third World**. Monticello, Ill.: Vance Bibliographies, n.d. 98 p. (Public Administration Series: Bibliography P-1063)

Arranged by country under the following divisions: general; political; economic; social; and natural resources. References to items dealing with Puerto Rico appear in each of the first four sections. Unannotated.

1.077.   Mitchell, Martha et al. **A Comprehensive Bibliography of Selected Ethnic Groups**. Indianapolis: Indiana State Department of Public Instruction, 1978. 118 p. (ED 191 782)

Attempts to list "books that would give researchers an accurate view of the histories of various ethnic groups." The section on Puerto Rico lists books under different topics. Readers should check the spelling of Spanish names and titles as frequent errors occur.

1.078.   Monteforte Toledo, Mario.   **Bibliografía sociopolítica latinoamericana**. Mexico: Universidad Autónoma de Mexico, 1968. 157 p.

Represents a record of materials in Mexican libraries to the date of publication. The Puerto Rican section contains a mixed bag of seventeen annotated entries. Only author, title and date of publication are given in the citations.

1.079.   Morales Travieso, María Victoria and Elena Giráldez Rodríguez. **Bibliografía sobre Puerto Rico**. La Habana, Cuba: Biblioteca Nacional José Martí, Departamento de Investigaciones Bibliográficas, 1984. 116 p.

Although cited in Loroña, (1.071, 1985-86), no copy of this work was obtained for examination.

1.080.   Munden, Kenneth and Milton Greenbaum. **Records of the Bureau of Insular Affairs Relating to Puerto Rico, 1898-1934; A List of Selected Files**. Washington, D.C.: 1943. 47 p. (National Archives. Special List, no.4)

> This is a subject-arranged list of materials relating to Puerto Rico in the National Archives. File numbers are indicated after each topic. A general introduction explains the work of the Bureau in Puerto Rico and the organization and content of the work.

1.081.   **NACLA'S Bibliography on Latin America**. New York: North American Congress on Latin America, 1973. 48 p.

> The "focus is anti-imperialist and preference is given to writers on the left." Puerto Rico is represented by sixteen entries with cross references to three additional sources. Briefly annotated.

1.082.   New York Public Library. **Dictionary Catalog of the Research Libraries of the New York Public Library**. New York: 1972-

> Produced by computer, this source records materials that form part of the Library's collection. Volume 601 has entries under "Puerto Rican...", "Puerto Ricans", and "Puerto Rico." Other volumes can be consulted for specific works or other special topics with Puerto Rico as a subheading.

1.083.   _____. **Dictionary Catalog of the Schomburg Collection of Negro Literature and History**. 9 vols. Boston: G. K. Hall, 1962; **Supplement**. 6 vols. Boston: G. K. Hall, 1967-1972.

> This book catalog of a collection which specializes in Negro life and history includes materials on Puerto Rico in the seventh volume. Other related references can be found throughout the catalog. An important location tool.

1.084.   _____. Reference Department. **Dictionary Catalog of the History of the Americas**. 28 vols. Boston: G. K. Hall, 1961; .First Supplement. 9 vols. 1974.

> The holdings of an important specialized collection are reflected in this book catalog. Volume nineteen has entries under "Puerto Rican..." and "Puerto Rico."

1.085.   New York State Education Department, Albany.   Bureau of
Bilingual Education. **An Annotated Bibliography on Materials on the
Puerto Rican and Mexican Cultures**. Albany, N.Y.: 1982. 115 p.

> Intended to serve school personnel working with bilingual students or
> those for whom English is a second language. The section on Puerto
> Rico gives full bibliographic data and annotations for over 200 items
> written in English and Spanish. Grade levels are indicated. Many items
> are identified as being of general interest or of an adult level. The
> lack of an index tends to reduce the usefulness of the work.

1.086.   Okinshevich, Leo, comp. **Latin America in Soviet Writings:
A Bibliography**. Edited by Robert G. Carlton. 2 vols. Baltimore, Md.: The
Johns Hopkins Press, 1966. (Hispanic Foundation Publications, 1)

> The first volume describes books and articles on Latin America
> published in the Soviet Union from 1917 to 1958, while volume two
> covers from 1959 to 1964. Both include material on Puerto Rico,
> with emphasis on politics and government. English titles are given.
> Indexes facilitate the use of this source which supersedes an earlier
> work of the same title.

1.087.   Ortiz Corps, Edgardo.   "Indice bibliográfico puertorriqueño."
Exegesis: Revista del Colegio Universitario de Humacao. Vol. 1,
1986/87-

> Each issue includes a bibliographical section on books and journal
> articles published on different topics relating to Puerto Rico. Many
> issues show a marked preference for scientific publications.

1.088.   Palau y Dulcet, Antonio. **Manual del librero hispano-
americano; bibliografía general española e hispano-americana
desde la invención de la imprenta hasta nuestros tiempos, con el
valor comercial de los impresos descritos**. 2d rev. ed. Barcelona,
Spain: Librería Palau, 1948-

> A useful, retrospective source originally published between 1923 and
> 1927. It attempts to be a complete listing of Spanish and Latin
> American publications. It is organized alphabetically by author (or
> title, in the case of anonymous works). Many references to Puerto
> Rico can be found using the index volumes. Specific topics, persons,
> and towns can also be searched.

1.089.   Pasarell, Emilio. "Enmiendas y adiciones a la lista alfabética de
periódicos que se inserta en la obra del Doctor Pedreira titulada 'El

periodismo en Puerto Rico'." **Historia** n.s. 2 (July-December 1963): 99-103.

> This work adds new titles and makes corrections in the information given in Pedreira's ample listing (1.092). For each entry the title of the newspaper, place and date of publication, and names of the directors are given when available. Psarell was a well-respected scholar and intellectual.

1.090.   Pedreira, Antonio S. **Bibliografía puertorriqueña, 1493-1930.** Madrid: Imprenta de la Librería y Casa Editorial Hernando, 1932. 707 p.; **New York:** Burt Franklin Reprints, 1974.   (Monografías de la Universidad de Puerto Rico, Series A: Estudios hispánicos, no.1)

> Material for this unparalleled, comprehensive bibliograpy was collected over a period of seven years. References are cited alpha-betically under each of ten major subjects, each of which is further subdivided by topics: bibliographical sources; general information; natural history; health; social economy; political and administrative history; cultural organization; history of Puerto Rico; literary history; and various topics. Some entries are repeated under various subjects. Pedriera includes citations to articles appearing in the following important journals: **Boletín de la Asociación Médica de Puerto Rico** (1903-1930); **Boletín Histórico de Puerto Rico** (1914-1930); **Journal of the Department of Agriculture of Porto Rico; Revista de Agricultura de Puerto Rico; Revista de las Antillas; Revista de Obras Públicas de Puerto Rico; Revista Puertorriqueña; Porto Rico Health Review; Puerto Rico Ilustrado** (1910-1930); and **The Puerto Rico Herald.** Literary articles and poetry published in the aforementioned journals are not cited. Nor does Pedreira include newspaper articles, manuscripts, prayer books, abstract materials of little historical value, ordinances, municipal reports and budgets, and regulations of casinos, churches, societies, sugar refineries or other such institutions. Two important features must be pointed out because of their usefulness: the local history section of part eight on the history of Puerto Rico cites references alphabetically under the names of each town; and, the Puerto Rican biography section of part nine on literary history first lists works of collective biography then indexes them alphabetically by biographee. The latter is the first tool of its kind ever made available. The book has author and subject indexes as well as an appendix of publications appearing or found after the bibliography had been completed.

1.091.   Pedreira, Antonio S. **Curiosidades literarias de Puerto Rico**. San Juan, P.R.: Biblioteca de Autores Puertorriqueños, 1939. 48 p.

A rather informal work which gives bibliographical information on books, pamphlets and magazines published in Puerto Rico or by Puerto Ricans. It includes information on the first libraries, printing presses, newspapers, books, and other such things or achievements.

1.092.   _____ **El periodismo en Puerto Rico**. La Habana, Cuba: Imprenta Ucar, García y Cía., 1941. 470 p.; Río Piedras, P.R.: Editorial Edil, 1969. 558 p. (Monografías de la Universidad de Puerto Rico. Series A. Estudios Hispánicos, no. 3)

A detailed study of journalism in Puerto Rico which includes a bibliography of newspapers published on the island (pages 387 to 558). In addition to the newspaper title, all available details are provided: town of publication, type of publication, directors or proprietors, and a history of the publication. See Emilio Pasarell's "Enmiendas y adiciones a la lista alfabética de periódicos..."(1.089) for an update to this work.

1.093.   Pérez de Rosa, Albertina. "Las bibliografías puertorriqueñas." **Boletín de la Sociedad de Bibliotecarios de Puerto Rico** 3 (January-April 1964): 7-17.

An historical, bibliographic essay which discusses the relative importance and merits of bibliographies compiled from the 1880's to the 1960's. Some bibliographies on special topics are also considered. See also Gonzalo Velázquez's "La bibliografía en Puerto Rico" (1.125) for a similar study.

1.094.   Pineiro, Gladys. **A Puerto Rican Bibliography**. San José, Calif.: San José State University Library, 1973. 84 p.

A subject-arranged bibliography of books, journal articles and government publications on Puerto Rico and Puerto Ricans in the United States. Includes an introductory essay on the history of Puerto Rico.

1.095.   "Puerto Rican Books in Translation." In **Latin American Masses and Minorities: Their Images and Realities, edited by** Seminar on the Acquisition of Latin American Library Materials (30th: 1985: Princton, N.J.) , vol.2, 564-69. Madison, Wisc.: SALALM Secretariat, 1987.

No author or introduction is given for this listing of forty-three books on Puerto Rico. Each reference is followed by the complete citation to the translation to English or Spanish, as the case may be. All subject fields are represented.

1.096.   "Puerto Rico: Puerto Rican Authors; A Sampling of Books Available in Spanish." **Branch Library Book News** (New York Public Library) 46 (October 1968): 3-11.

Author, title and a brief comment are provided for each of roughly 144 items. The list is organized alphabetically under broad subject categories. Updates a 1963 list.

1.097.   Puerto Rico. Departamento de Instrucción Pública. Servicio de Bibliotecas Públicas. Proyecto Cooperación Interbibliotecaria. "Catálogo [de la] Sala Puertorriqueña [de la] Biblioteca Pública Carnegie." Hato Rey, P.R.: 1982? 364 p. (photocopy)

A photocopy of the shelf list of the Puerto Rican Collection of the Carnegie Library in San Juan, perhaps the oldest-existing public library on the island. The arrangement is by Dewey Decimal Classi-fication number, followed by a section of biographies. This catalog was reproduced as part of a Title III project on interlibrary coopera-tion by the Department of Education, the agency which is responsible for public libraries in Puerto Rico. An important finding tool.

1.098.   _____ Junta de Planificación. "Inventario de estudios realizados por algunas agencias e instituciones gubernamentales." San Juan, P.R.: 1973. 534 p.

Earnhardt cited this as a work in draft version (2.319, pp. 100-101).

1.099.   Rivera, Guillermo.   **A Tentative Bibliography of the Belles-Lettres of Porto Rico.** Cambridge, Mass.: Harvard University Press, 1931. 61 p.

Unannotated entries are roughly classified under topics such as: anthologies; art; bibliography; criticism; drama; essay; history; legend; novel; oratory; poetry and short story; unclassified; writings in periodicals, collections, etc.; incomplete or doubtful titles drawn from different sources; periodicals; and a special bibliography on Hostos. References are often incomplete or cited in different formats. Entries may appear under several headings. Some errors in author and/or title or classification occur. The section on Hostos is rather poor. No index.

1.100.   Sable, Martin H. **A Guide to Latin American Studies**. 2
vols. Los Angles, Calif.: Latin American Center, University of California,
1967.

>   A selective interdisciplinary bibliography with approximately 5,000
>   annotations. It is arranged alphabetically by subject with topical and
>   geographical subheadings. Subject and author indexes are included at
>   the end of the second volume. References can be found under "Puerto
>   Rico", "Puerto Rican..." and on specific topics.

1.101.   Sáez Estades, Mercedes. **Bibliografía anotada: revistas y
periódicos de Puerto Rico en el siglo XIX**. San Juan, P.R.: Sociedad de
Bibliotecarios de Puerto Rico, 1974. 41, 4 p.

>   An annotated guide to nineteenth century magazines and newspapers,
>   copies of which are still in existence. Gives as much information as
>   is available: place of publication, duration, directors and collabora-
>   tors, type of article and audience. Sáez also specifies the number of
>   issues available and their physical condition.

1.102.   Sama, Manuel María. **Bibliografía puerto-rriqueña**.
Mayagüez, P.R.: Tipografía Comercial, 1887. 159 p.

>   Based on the author's personal collection, this commendable,
>   pioneering effort is organized chronologically to show the "slow
>   progress" of Puerto Rican bibliography. Except for literary works,
>   brief descriptions of each item's contents are given. Sama admitted
>   that the work was incomplete since he excluded government reports,
>   school texts and other works not in his possession. The 250 works
>   cited were written by Puerto Ricans or on Puerto Rican topics. The
>   introduction includes statistics on the number of works by date, by
>   city of publication, by subjects and by author. Illustrated with
>   portraits and biographical data of important authors. A title index
>   concludes the work.

1.103.   Senior, Clarence and Josefina de Román. "A Selected
Bibliography on Puerto Rico and the Puerto Ricans." New York: Department
of Labor, 1951. 32 p. (mimeographed)

>   Although this bibliography lacks an introduction, most of its
>   references are briefly annotated. It is arranged alphabetically under
>   the following headings: the Puerto Rican migrant; background-
>   historical and descriptive; economic, social and health conditions;
>   reconstruction program and labor; education; politics and public
>   administration; fiction, children's books, poetry and films; music;

cookery; bibliogrphies; sources of further information. Some
Spanish-language sources are included. (Also reprinted in **The
Puerto Ricans: Migration and General Bibliography**. New
York: Arno Press, 1975)

1.104.   Sociedad Puertorriqueña de Escritores. **Catálogo de libros de
la Biblioteca Dr. Manuel Alonso de la Sociedad Puertorriqueña de
Escritores**. [San Juan, P.R.: 19?] 76 p.

An author listing of books in the library. Provides only author and
titles. Includes some Puerto Rican works but one must know the
author's nationality in order to identify them. Mainly of historical
interest.

1.105.   Szwed, John F. and Roger D. Abrahams. **Afro-American Folk
Culture: An Annotated Bibliography of Materials from North,
Central and South America and the West Indies**. 2 vols. Philadelphia:
Institiute for the Study of Human Issues, 1978. (814 p.) (Bibliographical
and Special Series, v. 31)

Describes published material on Afro-American folk culture. The
second volume has a section on Puerto Rico (pages 599 to 604) where
cross references are also made to items in other sections. Forty-two
books and journal articles in English and Spanish are cited. Indexes
facilitate the book's use.

1.106.   Toro, Josefina del. **A Partial Bibliography of Puerto Rican
Publications for 1938**. Washington, D.C.:   The Inter-American Book
Exchange, 1940. 7 p.

A simple listing of items published during 1938. Cites books,
government documents and some journals.

1.107.   Torres, Víctor, comp. **Indice del material bibliográfico
sobre Puerto Rico, en el 'Educational Resources Information
Center (ERIC)', 1975-1980**. Río Piedras, P.R.: Colección de Referencia,
Sistema de Bibliotecas, Universidad de Puerto Rico, Recinto de Río Piedras,
1986. 49 p. (**Boletín bibliográfico**, serie A, no. 13-1)

A commendable contribution to identifying material related to Puerto
Rico in the ERIC files for the years 1975 to 1980. Arranged
alphaberically by author with a subject index. References for the
subject headings are to ERIC numbers, not authors. Also contains a
bilingual guide to relevant subject headings in ERIC. Covers all
subjects.

1.108.   Torres, Víctor. **Indice del material bibliográfico sobre Puerto Rico en 'Resources in Education', 1981-1985**. Río Piedras, P.R.: Colección de Referencia, Sistema de Bibliotecas, Universidad de Puerto Rico, Recinto de Río Piedras, 1988. 32 p.

>   Updates the previous title. However, it is arranged by document number with a subject index. An English-Spanish list of subject headings is appended.

1.109.   Torres Alamo, Leida Iris. **La realidad de Puerto Rico: bibliografía de las tésis presentadas en la U.P.R. Recinto de Río Piedras de 1929 a 1972**. Río Piedras, P.R.: 1973. 126 p.

>   Prepared for a library science course, this bibliography covers masters and doctoral theses dealing with the social, economic and political conditions of Puerto Rico. Organized by faculty then alphabetically under each department. Indexes by faculty, author, title and subject.

1.110.   Trelles y Govin, Carlos M. **Ensayo de bibliografía cubana de los siglos XVII y XVIII, seguido de unos apuntes para la bibliografía dominicana y puertorriqueña**. Matanzas, Cuba: Imprenta "El Escritorio", 1907. xi, 228, xxviii p.

>   This descriptive bibliography of Cuban materials includes references to eighteen items published in or about Puerto Rico. Brief information is given for several of the authors. The seventy-six page supplement,published in 1908, has scattered references to Puerto Rico in the fourth section.

1.111.   United States. Library of Congress. Division of Bibliography. **A List of Books (With References to Periodicals) on Porto Rico**. By A. P. C. Griffin. Washington, D.C.: Government Printing Office, 1901. 55 p.

>   "It embodies a considerable collection of native literature gathered by Dr. Friedenwald upon the occasion of a visit to the island in 1898." Includes only items owned by the library. Some entries have contents notes. (Also reprinted in: **The Puerto Ricans: Migration and General Bibliography**. New York: Arno Press, 1975)

1.112.   _____ _____ _____ **Puerto Rico: A Selected List of Recent References**. Compiled by Ana Duncan Brown under the direction of Florence S. Hellman. Washington, D.C.: 1943. 44 p.

Intended as a supplement to the library's typewritten list which was prepared near the end of the 1930s but is not readily available. Only the "more outstanding publications are repeated." About 381 references to Puerto Rico are arranged by topic: bibliographies; general description and travel; economic and social conditions; education; industry, resources and commerce; politics and government; and defense. A list of abbreviations is appended.

1.113.   United States.   Library of Congress.   General Reference and Bibliography Division.   **Non Self-Governing Areas; with Special Emphasis on Mandates and Trusteeships: A Selected List of References.**   2 vols.   Compiled by Helen F. Conover.   Washington, D.C.: 1947.

References to Puerto Rico can be found in the subject index.

1.114.   _____.   Superintendent of Documents.   **United States Public Documents Relating to the Non-contiguous Territory and to Cuba.**   Washington, D.C.: 1910-1936.

Title varies. Also published as **Insular Possessions; Guam, Philippines, Puerto Rico, Samoa, Virgin Islands...** Includes information on works relating to Puerto Rico and published within the time period indicated.

1.115.   Universidad de Puerto Rico. Centro de Investigaciones Sociales. **Bibliografía puertorriqueña de ciencias sociales.**   Río Piedras, P.R.: 1977. 600 p.

A commendable effort at recording materials published from 1931 to 1960. Although the emphasis is on the social sciences, other fields are also represented. Those not covered are law and jurisprudence, literature and natural sciences. The bibliography is based on the Center's card catalog and a CIDOC bibliography on the language issue (2.169). As recognized in the book's introduction, the major problem of this publication is its organization. Part one covers 1931 to 1954, while part two deals with material published from 1954 to 1960. Each part is arranged by major fields. Entries are not duplicated under various classifications. The principle sections include: bibliographical sources, general works, nature, towns and regions, society and culture before the nineteenth century, the nineteenth century and the twentieth century. The lack of a good general index greatly hampers the use of this publication. Partially updated by the Center's annual reports.

1.116.   Universidad de Puerto Rico.   Oficina de Coordinación de
Investigaciones. "Inventario de las tesis realizadas y en preparación
existentes en el Recinto Universitario de Río Piedras hasta el mes de enero
de 1974." Río Piedras, P.R.: 1974. 133 p. (mimeographed)

> Arranged alphabetically by faculty, then department, then author. The
> information included varies according to the faculty that submitted
> it. An earlier edition of 111 leaves was issued in June of 1973.
> Covers all disciplines.

1.117.   _____. Recinto Universitario de Mayagüez.   Biblioteca
General. **Colección de tesis y tesinas**. Rev. ed. Mayagüez, P.R.: 1977.
141 p.

> Lists theses held by the Library of the University of Puerto Rico's
> Mayagüez Campus. Although it is organized by Dewey Decimal number,
> there are author and subject indexes. The majority of theses de-
> scribed were presented in Mayagüez, but the list does include some
> from other universities. The Mayagüez campus is especially well-
> known for its engineering and agricultural science programs. This
> bibliography replaces earlier editions. A supplement was published in
> 1978.

1.118.   _____. Sistema de Bibliotecas. **Repertorio colectivo de
periódicos en Puerto Rico: lista preliminar de periódicos en la
Biblioteca José M. Lázaro de la Universidad de Puerto Rico. Union
List of Newspapers in Puerto Rico: First Part: Preliminary List
of Newspapers in the José M. Lázaro Library of the University of
Puerto Rico**. Río Piedras, P.R.: 1986. 27 p.

> Part of a project funded by the National Endowment for the Humani-
> ties, this is a title listing of Puerto Rican and American newspapers
> owned by the Library, the largest on the island. No holdings or facts
> of publication are given. For more complete details see the next
> entry (1.119).

1.119.   _____. _____. **Repertorio colectivo de periódicos
en Puerto Rico: lista preliminar de periódicos en las
instituciones participantes. Union List of Newspapers in Puerto
Rico: Preliminary List of Newspapers in the Participating
Institutions**. Río Piedras, P.R.: 1986. 67 p.

> This union list is the result of a project funded by the National En-
> dowment for the Humanities to establish and develop a center for the
> bibliographic control, preservation and dissemination of newspapers

in Puerto Rico. The introduction defines the term newspaper with
regard to content, audience and format. The main body of the work is
an alphabetical title list of Puerto Rican newspapers. Information on
subtitle, place of publication, libraries holding copies and dates of
issues owned is also supplied. Another short section cites American
newspapers received in Puerto Rican libraries. A list of initials for
participating libraries is included.

1.120.   University of Florida Libraries, Gainesville, Florida. **Caribbean
Acquisitions: Materials Acquired by the University of Florida.**
Gainesville, Fla.: University of Florida, 1957/58–

An annual list of "material acquired under the Farmington plan and
from the University's emphasis on Latin American studies." It is
arranged by subject with geographic subdivisions when the amount of
material merits it. Numerous entries of interest for the study of
Puerto Rico can be found in each yearly catalog.

1.121.   _____ **Catalog of the Latin American Collection.** 13
vols. Boston: G. K. Hall, 1973; **First Supplement.** 7 vols. 1980.

An author-subject catalog of 120,000 items in the university's Latin
American Collection. Volume eleven has entries beginning with
"Puerto Rican" and "Puerto Rico." Other relevant references can be
found under specific headings with Puerto Rico as a subdivision. A
helpful location tool.

1.122.   University of Texas Library, Austin. Latin American Collection.
Catalog of the Latin American Collection. 31 vols. Boston: G. K. Hall,
1969; **First Supplement.** 5 vols. 1971.

This reproduction of the library catalog of a major Latin American
collection (approximately 175,000 items) includes materials on
Puerto Rico. Most of them can be found in volume twenty-four
although other entries can be found under specific subject headings.
Various multivolume supplements have been published. Continued by
the **Catalog of the Nettie Lee Benson Latin American
Collection.** An important aid for locating copies of books on Puerto
Rico.

1.123.   Vázquez, Lourdes. "New Puerto Rican Bibliography." **SALALM
Newsletter** 12 (June 1985): 3–4.

An unannotated list of forty-six bibliographies published before 1985.
A useful and well-chosen listing.

1.124. Velázquez, Gonzalo, comp. **Anuario bibliográfico puertorriqueño; índice alfabético de libros, folletos, revistas y periódicos publicados en Puerto Rico...** Río Piedras, P. R.: Biblioteca General, Universidad de Puerto Rico, 1949-

> A unique attempt to record annually and systematically the bibliographic production of Puerto Rico. However, annual cumulations were always delayed, often by several years. Velázquez tried to record all works written in or about Puerto Rico or published by Puerto Ricans anywhere in the world. Complete bibliographic information appears under the main entry with only limited information under added entries such as subject, editor, and title. All entries appear in one alphabetical sequence. The annual includes pamphlets, government documents, journals and newspapers as well as books. Each volume has lists of printers, publishers, bookstores (by towns), and abbreviations. The last volume published corresponded to 1973/74.

1.125. _____ "La bibliografía en Puerto Rico." In **Seminario piloto de bibliografía: informe final**, edited by Seminario Bibliográfico de Centro América y el Caribe, 60-66. La Habana, Cuba: Agrupación Bibliográfica Cubana José Toribio Medina, 1955.

> Originally an oral presentation, this bibliographic essay traces the history of Puerto Rican bibliography from earliest times to 1948 when the author's **Anuario biliográfico puertorriqueño** was first published. Velázquez assesses the importance, merits and weaknesses of each general bibliography published during that period. He also suggests a plan of action for ensuring an adequate record of Puerto Rico's bibliographic production Unfortunately, neither this plan nor an acceptable substitute have been implemented.

1.126. _____ **Biblioteca de obras puertorriqueñas**. New York: New York Public Library, 1973.

> This work was cited by Lourdes Vázquez (1.123). However, the author was unable to locate a copy for examination.

1.127. Vivó, Paquita, ed. **The Puerto Ricans: An Annotated Bibliography**. New York: R.R. Bowker, 1973. 299 p.

> One of the most widely-recognized and often-consulted works of recent decades. It was prepared to "offer light to Puerto Ricans in search of their own roots and their cultural heritage...[and to] serve as a resource to non-Puerto Ricans...who should and do want to know about their fellow citizens." Therefore, wherever possible,

preferenceis given to English-language sources and latest editions.
Wide in scope, the work is organized into four main parts: books,
pamphlets and dissertations arranged alphabetically under twenty-
one subject headings; government documents, both Puerto Rican and
federal; periodical literature, including a list of selected periodical
titles and a section of references to specific journal articles;
audiovisual materials, including motion pictures and filmstrips.
Brief annotations accompany most entries, generally stating the
scope of the item and its central thesis. Oftentimes the author's
background or authority is specified. Annotations are generally not
evaluative, except for works of juvenile literature. Indexes are by
subject, author, and title. Use of the subject index is highly
recommended.

1.128.   Vivó, Paquita. "Reading and Viewing: An Introduction to Recent
Works about Puerto Rico." **Civil Rights Digest** 6 (Winter 1973): 39-40.

In this short bibliographical essay on English-language sources, Vivó
attempts to identify materials that will "help readers understand not
only the complexities and problems surrounding the approximately
1.5 million Puerto Ricans who live in the United States, but also the
history, culture and literature of the Puerto Rican community as a
whole.

1.129.   Ward, J. H. **Bibliografía de revistas puertorriqueñas
1967-1968.** College Station, Tex.: Texas A & M University, 1969.

Although cited in **Anuario bibliográfico puertorriqueño** (1.124)
for 1969-70, no copy of this work was obtained.

1.130.   **Year Book of Caribbean Research: Survey of Research
and Investigation in Caribbean Commission Territories; 1948-**
Port-of-Spain, Trinidad: Research Branch, Central Secretariat, Caribbean
Commission, 1949-

A subject bibliography of scientific and social science research
carried out in the Caribbean. For each entry, the agency, title of the
project, and names of the investigators are given, as is a short
description of the project and its initiation and completion dates.
The index of research projects by geographic area permits easy
access to material related to the island. The 1949 supplement
includes a selective bibliography. Only issue examined.

1.131.   Zimmerman, Irene. **A Guide to Current Latin American Periodicals: Humanities and Social Sciences**. 2d ed. Gainesville, Fla.: Kallman, 1961. 357 p.

>   This annotated bibliography of Latin American periodicals includes a section of fifteen Puerto Rican titles (pages 182-86). A new edition would prove very useful.

Special Topics

2.001.   Babín, María Teresa.   "Bibliografía general sobre las artes plásticas en Puerto Rico." **Educación** 13 (August 1963): 124-26.

An unannotated bibliography of twenty-eight references to the plastic arts in Puerto Rico. The compiler is a well-known author and critic. Selective.

2.002.   **Bibliografía musical puertorriqueña**.   San Juan, P.R.: Instituto de Cultura Puertorriqueña, 1981. 9 p.

No indication is given of the compiler's name nor of the scope and purpose of the bibliography. It appears to be a selected list of works written on Puerto Rican music and musicians. For a more complete work see Figueroa's bibliography (2.006).

2.003.   Chevrette, Valerie.   **Annotated Bibliography of the Precolumbian Art and Archaeology of the West Indies.** New York: Museum of Primitive Art, 1971. 18 p. (Primitive Art Bibliographies, 9)

Brief descriptions accompany thirty-four entries pertaining to Puerto Rico. Additional references may be found in the general and the discovery and early accounts sections.

2.004.   Colegio Universitario de Cayey. Biblioteca. Departamento de Servicios al Público. Sala de Referencia. "Bibliografía mínima selectiva sobre la música puertorriqueña." Cayey, P.R.: 1980. 6 p. (mimeographed)

A selective listing of books, journal and newspaper articles, and
miscellaneous material on Puerto Rican music. Works about
individual composers or musicians are not included.

2.005.   Colón Jiménez, Elvira. **Indice bibliográfico: arte; 'Revista
Puerto Rico Ilustrado,' 1910-1920.** San Juan, P.R.: Sociedad Amigos
del Museo de la Universidad de Puerto Rico in collaboration with the Centro
de Estudios Avanzados de Puerto Rico y el Caribe, 1983. 87 p.

Adapted from the author's thesis, this annotated bibliography includes
articles, chronicles, reviews, photographs, caricatures, drawings,
illustrations for literary works, and professional or commercial
advertisements published in one of Puerto Rico's most important
magazines, **Puerto Rico Ilustrado**, from 1910 to 1920. A list of
pseudonyms is included as an appendix.

2.006.   Figueroa de Thompson, Annie. **An Annotated Bibliography of
Writings about Music in Puerto Rico.** Ann Arbor, Mich.: Music Library
Association, 1975 (c1974). 71 p.

Arranged alphabetically by author, the work covers books, theses and
journal articles. Annotations give brief descriptions of the contents
of each entry, the author's point of view and/or whether the item is a
formal or informal study. The most recent reference is to a work
published in 1972. The index allows for access by subject, musician,
genre and title. A Spanish-language translation, **Bibliografía
anotada de la música en Puerto Rico**, was published in San Juan
by the Institute of Puerto Rican Culture in 1977.

2.007.   **Handbook of Latin American Art.   Manual de arte
latinoamericano: A Bibliographic Compilation**. General editor: Joyce
Wadell Bailey. Santa Barbara, Calif.: ABC-Clio Information Services, 1984-

The first part of the first volume includes specific references to
Puerto Rico in the general references section (pages 100 to 102) and
in that of the 19th and 20th centuries (pages 450 to 466). The latter
is further subdivided by topics and/or media. Volume two, **Art of
the Colonial Period**, also covers Puerto Rico (pages 185 to 204).
Citations to artists are included, as well as references to specific art
forms, museums, media , urban planning and other such topics.

2.008.   Louie de Irizarry, Florita Z. **The Architecture of Old San
Juan, Puerto Rico: A General Bibliography**. Monticello, Ill.: Vance
Bibliographies, 1983. 9 p. (Architecture Series: Bibliography A 1066)

Lists materials relating to the Spanish architecture of the island's capital city. Brief annotations supplement the citations.

2.009.　　Muñoz, María Luisa. "Bibliografía de la música." **Educación** 13 (August 1963): 121-23.

The author is well-known for a published history of Puerto Rican music. The present work is a list of thirty-two citations, some of which do not refer specifically to Puerto Rico. Unannotated.

2.010.　　Rivera de Figueroa, Carmen A. **Architecture for the Tropics: A Bibliographical Synthesis (con una versión castellana resumida: Arquitectura para el trópico)**. Río Piedras, P.R.: Editorial Universitaria, Universidad de Puerto Rico, 1980. 203 p.

Arranged in three main parts: man, climate and architecture; bibliography on architecture for the tropics: chronological development (by decade); architecture for the tropics: main aspects. Many references dealing with Puerto Rican themes can be found in the latter section. Each part has an introductory essay.

2.011.　　Thompson, Donald. "Music, Theater and Dance in Central America and the Caribbean: An Annotated Bibliography of Dissertations and Theses." **Revista/Review Interamericana** 9 (Spring 1979): 115-40.

Forty-four of the 126 items in this list deal with Puerto Rican dance, music and theater. Arranged alphabetically, each entry gives author, title, an indication of whether the work is a thesis or a dissertation, university, year and number of pages. A subject index increases the effectiveness of this work.

2.012.　　United States.　Library of Congress.　Division of Music. **Bibliography of Latin American Folk Music**.　Compiled by Gilbert Chase. New York: AMS Press, 1942. 141 p.

Fourteen references to Puerto Rican folk music are to be found on pages 115 to 117.

2.013.　　Universidad de Puerto Rico.　Escuela de Arquitectura. Biblioteca. "Colección Puertorriqueña: bibliografía." 2d. ed. Río Piedras, P.R.: 1982. 101 p. (mimeographed)

A subject listing of classified books in the library's collection. Although the emphasis is on architecture, the collection is a good, general one on the island and its people. No author or title indexes are provided.

BIO-BIBLIOGRAPHIES

2.014.   Alamo de Torres, Daisy. **Bibliografía de Ester Feliciano Mendoza (1935-1980).**   2d. rev. ed.   San Juan, P.R.:   Sociedad de Biblioterarios de Puerto Rico, 1980. 34 p. (Cuadernos bibliográficos, 2)

Following an introduction on the life and achievements of Ester Feliciano Mendoza, the first section of the bibliography describes works written by her. The second part lists material written on the author and her work. Feliciano Mendoza, recently deceased, was best known for her books written for children.

2.015.   Alegría, Félix L. "Luis Lloréns Torres: bibliografía." **Revista Hispánica Moderna** (New York) 19 (January-December 1953): 85-87.

This list of works by/about Luis Lloréns Torres is divided into four sections: editions of his works (six items); prologues (six items); studies on Lloréns (seventy-seven entries); and poems dedicated to him (seven items). No annotations.

2.016.   Arce de Vázquez, Margot. "Bibliografía de Manuel Zeno Gandía." **Asomante** 11 (October-December 1955): 72-74.

Arce, a widely-respected literary critic and author, prepared this unannotated listing to accompany an issue of the journal dedicated to Zeno Gandía. It describes the author's literary works but does not refer to items written about his work. It is arranged in the following sections: stories; novels; poetry; prose; and theater. The prose section is arranged chronologically under subheadings such as conferences, criticisms, and chronicles.

2.017.   _____."Bibliografía selecta." **Asomante** 22 (October-December 1966): 79-83.

A selective, unannotated bibliography of the prose and poetry of José de Diego which also cites eighty-one critical studies of his life and work. This list was prepared as part of an issue of **Asomante** dedicated to this famous Puerto Rican. Much of the material was taken from Arce's **La obra literaria de José de Diego**.

2.018.   Arriogotía, Luis de. "Bibliografía de Margot Arce de Vázquez." **Revista de Estudios Hispánicos** (Puerto Rico) 2 (January-December 1972): 283-92.

This work emphasizes works written by Arce de Vázquez with only a small section of fifty-six references to biographies and criticisms of her work. Arce's writings are described under the following sub-headings: editions, translations, articles, reviews and prologues. Unfortunately no annotations are included.

2.019.   Arroyo Martínez, Jossianna and Manuel de la Puebla. "Bibliografía." **Mairena** 7 (1985): 169-73.

Describes works written by and about Julia de Burgos, Puerto Rico's most loved female poet. Burgos lived in the United States for many years before her untimely death there. Of the eighty-one entries, seventy-four describe works of criticism or biography.

2.020.   "Bibliografía." **Mairena** 2 (Spring 1980): 95-99.

This bibliography covering works by and about the illustrious poet Evaristo Ribera Chevremont was taken from the book **El estilo de Evaristo Ribera Chevremont**, written by Alicea Fernández Gill. The first part cites Ribera's poetry, anthologies and works of prose (thirty-six references). The second section identifies twenty-nine works of criticism on the poet.

2.021.   "Bibliografía." **Mairena** 4 (Winter 1982): 181-88.

Francisco Matos Paoli is one of Puerto Rico's distinguished contemporary poets. His works, and the works of criticsm and evaluation which they have stimulated, are described in this bio-bibliography taken from the files of Isabel Freire de Matos. Cites fifty-six of the author's poetic and prose works, as well as twenty-six critical studies by different authors.

2.022.   "Bibliografía de Eugenio María de Hostos." **Boletín de la Biblioteca Ibero Americana de Bellas Artes** 2 (1939): 8-9.

The author was unable to locate a copy of this work which was cited by Foster (2.197).

2.023.   "Bibliografía de J. Benjamín Torres." **Revista del Colegio de Abogados de Puerto Rico** 48 (October-December 1987): 181-84.

Torres was a prominent researcher on Pedro Albizu Campos and the independence movement in Puerto Rico. This bibliography of his works is arranged by books, articles, book reviews, interviews, book reviews of his works, announcements and a portfolio. A total of fifty-three items are included. No annotations given.

2.024.   "Bibliografía de Luis Palés Matos." **La Torre** 8 (January-June 1960): 331-36.

Although a small section of published editions of the author's works is included, most of the references in this bibliography concern works written about the life and work of Palés Matos. Palés is the island's most famous author of Afro-Antillian poetry.

2.025.   "Bibliografía parcial del profesor Angel G. Quintero Rivera." **Revista del Colegio de Abogados de Puerto Rico** 48 (October-December 1987): 163-65.

No introduction precedes the entries which are divided into two sections: books and articles. The latter includes chapters in books written or edited by other authors. Because of the date of publication, this list does not include an important work published in 1988: **Patricios y plebeyos** (Río Piedras, P.R.: Huracán).

2.026.   Caraballo-Abreu, Daisy. "Bibliografía de Concha Meléndez." **La Torre** 32 (April-September 1984): 377-419.

Part one lists editions of works written by Meléndez, a very distinguished and frequently quoted author and critic. This section is grouped by genre. The second part of the bibliography is identified as a chronology and lists journal and newspaper articles written by Meléndez in chronological order. The third and last section has 196 alphabetical entries for studies and criticisms of the author and her work. This bibliography supplements a complete issue of **La Torre** concerned with Meléndez. It is an important contribution, although unannotated.

2.027.   _____ "La prosa de Luis Lloréns Torres." **Revista de Estudios Hispánicos** (Puerto Rico) 3-4 (1971): 81-91.

Unannotated, this bibliography lists the prose works of an important author and public figure. Entries are arranged alphabetically under the following headings: books (one item); prologues (six items); articles (282 items); and dialogues (eight items). The list ends with six references to studies on Lloréns.

2.028.   Colegio Universitario de Cayey. Biblioteca. "Bibliografía de artículos escritos por Don Miguel Meléndez Muñoz para **Puerto Rico Ilustrado** de 1910-1952." Cayey, P.R.: 1974. 30 p.

>   Miguel Meléndez Muñoz was an eminant journalist and author who wrote about his native town of Cayey as well as Puerto Rican culture and folklore in general. Listed in this bibliography are his many contributions to one of the most important magazines of the era. It is arranged chronologically by date of publication. A subject and/or title index would make this bibliography much more useful.

2.029.   _____. _____. **Bibliografía Juan Antonio Corretjer.** Cayey, P.R.: 1986. [6] , 15 p.

>   Supplemented by a biographical sketch, this bibliography describes works written by Corretjer together with criticisms of his work. All items can be found in the library.

2.030.   _____. _____. "Compilación bibliográfica sobre la vida y obra de la Dra. María Teresa Babín." Cayey, P.R.: 1977. [10 p.] (mimeographed)

>   A bio-bibliography of an important Puerto Rican author.

2.031.   _____. _____. **Compilación bibliográfica sobre la vida y obra del Dr. Agustín Stahl Stamm.** Cayey, P.R.: 1976. 20 p

>   A brief biographical sketch of this famous Puerto Rican naturalist introduces the bibliography. A location is given for each work cited by or about Stahl.

2.032.   _____. _____. "José de Diego: bibliografía mínima." Cayey, P.R.: 1983. 13 p. (mimeographed)

>   A selective bio-bibliography of an important patriot.

2.033.   Dalmau de Sánchez, María Mercedes. "Bibliografía de Emilio Díaz Valcarcel." **Revista de Estudios Hispánicos** (Puerto Rico) 3 (January-June 1973): 81-89.

>   Works by Díaz Valcarcel (sixty-five items), criticisms of his works (fifty-four items) and miscelleneous information (seventeen entries) to 1976 (due to delays in the journal's publication) are compiled in this list. In her introduction, Dalmau explains Díaz Valcarcel's place and importance in Puerto Rican literature. She also lists the sources

consulted and difficulties encountered. A brief appendix lists
references supplied by Díaz but not verified by the compiler.

2.034.   Encarnación, Angel. "Francisco Matos Paoli, la poesía como
constancia de la existencia." **Revista de Estudios Hispánicos** (Puerto
Rico) 8 (1980): 181-99.

Descriptions of Matos Paoli's life and literary production precede the
bibliography. In the first section, works written by the poet are
organized chronologically by editions, individual poems, prose works
and unpublished works. The second section contains criticisms of
Matos's work: reviews, critical articles and theses.

2.035.   Fernández, Margarita. "Bibliografía anotada sobre Myrna Baez."
Imagen 4 (June 1980): 14-18.

A short, critical bibliography of an important contemporary Puerto
Rican artist. The arrangement is chronological under each of the
following headings: books and catalogs; journal articles; and newspaper articles.

2.036.   González Vélez, Isaura et al. **Jaime Benítez: bibliografía
selectiva.**   Mayagüez, P.R.:   Universidad de Puerto Rico, Recinto
Universitario de Mayagüez, Biblioteca General, 1989. 13 p. (Serie de
bibliografías ocasionales, 19)

Jaime Benítez is an important scholar who was also president of the
University of Puerto Rico for many years. The first part of this list
describes publications and speeches made by Benítez (eighty-three
entries). The second section cites over 100 books, articles and other
references written about this important public figure.

2.037.   Hernández Toledo, Ana Luz and Carlos Pérez Morales. **Tras las
huellas de Julia de Burgos: perfil bibliográfico.** With the collaboration of Dr. Juan Antonio Rodríguez Pagán. Humacao, P.R.: Universidad de
Puerto Rico, Colegio Universitario de Humacao, Biblioteca, Colección
Puerto-rriqueña, 1987. 15 p.

A bibliography of material by/about the famous poet. Not all items
cited can be found in the Library.

2.038.   Hernández Vargas, Nélida. "Luis Rafael Sánchez: guía bibliográfica." **Revista de Estudios Hispánicos** (Puerto Rico) 5 (1978): 167-
96.

This bibliography covers published and unpublished works of an important contemporary dramatist and author. It also includes criticisms, biographies, interviews and general studies about the author, as well as a selected list of productions of his dramas. The most complete compilation available.

2.039.   Hostos, Adolfo de. **Indice hemero-bibliográfico de Eugenio María de Hostos (incluye material inédito, iconografía y hostosiana), 1863-1940.** San Juan, P.R.: 1940. 756 p.

Works written about the illustrious patriot, Eugenio María de Hostos, as well as works written by him are cited in this exhaustive bibliography. A third section of the bibliography is an extensive listing of all illustrations, photographs, and other miscellaneous materials. While this was the most complete bibliography at the date of publication, it must now be supplemented by other works in order to find more recent studies that Hostos continues to inspire. The definitive work has yet to be compiled.

2.040.   Hostos, Eugenio Carlos de. **Eugenio María de Hostos, Promoter of Pan Americanism: A Collection of Writings and a Bibliography.** Madrid: Imp. Litografía y Encuadernación, 1953. 311 p.

Includes an ample bibliography of works written by Eugenio María de Hostos (pages 273 to 277) and of "hostosiana" (pages 278 to 311).

2.041.   "Juan Antonio Corretjer: bibliografía." **Reintegro** special issue 3 (August-December 1983): 14.

Works by Corretjer and published in the newspaper **El Mundo** are listed chronologically from 1945 to 1968. Corretjer was an important poet and independence advocate.

2.042.   López Morales, Humberto.   Aproximación a la bibliografía lingüística de Augusto Malaret." **Boletín de la Academia Puertorriqueña de la Lengua Española** 10 (1982): 37-46.

Noting that the work of Puerto Rico's most eminent linguist has yet to be studied with the attention and interest it deserves, López examines the shortcomings of existing compilations and the factors that have contributed to them. He then cites all of Malaret's works in chronological order with some brief comments or references to reviews of some works. A list of abbreviations is included for journal titles.

2.043.   Lugo Marichal, Flavia. "Bibliografía." **Sin Nombre** 4 (April–June 1974): 105-110.

This unannotated listing was prepared to accompany an issue dedicated to the study of Emilio S. Belaval. The first of two parts describes works written by the author. These are arranged chronologically under genre: short story collections (six items); stories published in **Puerto Rico Ilustrado** (twenty-seven entries); drama (ten works); essays, articles and literary criticisms (forty-four items). Twenty-five works written about Belaval are listed in the second section.

2.044.   "Manuel Rodríguez Ramos: bibliografía." **Revista del Colegio de Abogados de Puerto Rico** 33 (November 1972): 447-49.

Chronological bibliography of the works of Rodríguez Ramos, a Puerto Rican lawyer and law professor.

2.045.   Martínez de Hernández, Tomasita. **Bibliografía selectiva sobre la obra de Eneida B. Rivero**. Mayagüez, P.R.: Universidad de Puerto Rico, Recinto Universitario de Mayagüez, Biblioteca, 1985. 15 p.

Rivero was a well-known social scientist and professor at the Mayagüez Campus of the University of Puerto Rico. In addition to lists of Rivero's works and those written about her, this publication includes biographical information and a list of honors which she received.

2.046.   _____. **Germán Delgado Pasapera: bibliografía selectiva.** Mayagüez, P.R.: Universidad de Puerto Rico, Recinto Universitario de Mayagüez, 1985. 9 p.

Following a brief biographical sketch of the professor, author and historian, the compiler describes works written by him, arranged by format. A short section of references to material written about Delgado Pasapera is also included.

2.047.   Medina, Ramón Felipe. "Bibliografía esencial de Juan Antonio Corretjer: poesía (1924-1975)." **Mairena** 5 (Winter 1983): 49-58.

A chronologically arranged, unannotated bibliography which consists of the following sections: Corretjer's books of poetry; poetry in anthologies; reviews and criticisms of Corretjer's works, arranged by specific work; and general criticisms of his works. A short addendum updates the bibliography to 1983.

2.048.   Méndez Santos, Carlos. **Bibliografía de Carlos Méndez Santos, 1959-1979**. Ponce: Imprenta Universitaria, 1979. 46 p.

A detailed bibliography of the works of sociologist and university professor, Carlos Méndez Santos. The author has written a great deal on Puerto Rican customs and traditions and on his native city of Ponce, Puerto Rico. No index. A new edition is in preparation.

2.049.   Onís, Federico de. "Luis Palés Matos." **Islas; Revista de la Universidad Central de las Villas** (Santa Clara, Cuba) 1 (May/August 1959): 593-664.

After a lengthy discussion of the life and work of Palés, Onís offers a bibliography of works by Palés and studies on the poet. Some of Pales's poems can be found on the remaining pages of the article.

2.050.   Ortiz Guzmán, Rosaura. "Pedro Juan Soto: treinta años de producción literaria (1948-1978); guía bibliográfica." **Revista de Estudios Hispánicos** (Puerto Rico) 6 (1979): 251-83.

A biographical essay introduces this bibliography on the works of author Pedro Juan Soto. All editions of his works are cited by genre, including translations. A section of critical works includes theses, general studies, miscellaneous and activities and news items, written about Soto.

2.051.   Pedreira, Antonio S. "Bibliografía del Dr. Antonio S. Pedreira." **Isla** 2 (January 1940): 18-25.

This work was originally compiled by Pedreira himself. Rubén del Rosario organized it chronologically for publication in this issue dedicated to Pedreira. Rosario also included scattered comments within parenthesis. The first section cites thirty-two works on Pedreira. The next major part cites Pedreira's works in order of their publication. Under each work appear references to criticisms of each. The last section describes Pedreira's contributions to journals and newspapers as well as prologues written for works of other authors.

2.052.   _____ "Contribución al estudio de Hostos." **Alma Latina**, March 1931, pp. 47-50.

Bibliography of twenty titles written by Hostos and sixty-eight studies on the author and his works. Not annotated but authoritative.

2.053.   Pérez, Nélida and Amílcar Tirado. **Pedro Albizu Campos (1891-1965)**. New York: Centro de Estudios Puertorriqueños, Hunter College, City University of New York, 1986. 30 p.

> Bibliography of works written by/about Albizu. Includes a short biography by way of introduction.

2.054.   Pons de Alegría, Mela. "Ricardo E. Alegría: bibliografía cronológica." **Caribe** 3 (1982): 155-99.

> Profusely illustrated, this bibliography reflects the important contributions made by an eminent anthropologist and scholar who has also served as Director of the Institute of Puerto Rican Culture. The introduction supplies biographical information on Ricardo E. Alegría, including awards and honors received. The bibliography is arranged chronologically under the following headings: books; journal articles; newspaper articles; prologues and introductions to books, anthologies, and exhibition catalogs; notes; scripts for documentary films; and unpublished writings.

2.055.   Rivera, Félix, Amílcar Tirado and Nélida Pérez. **Julia de Burgos (1914-1953)**. New York: Centro de Estudios Puertorriqueños, Hunter College, City University of New York, 1986. 25 p.

> Biographical information about Julia de Burgos precedes a selective bibliography of material written by and about the poet. All materials can be found in the Centro Library.

2.056.   Rivera Cruz, Lourdes and Rita M. Seda de Rodríguez. **Eugenio María de Hostos: bibliografía selectiva**. Edited by Isaura González Vélez. Mayagüez, P.R.: Universidad de Puerto Rico, Recinto Universitario de Mayagüez, Biblioteca General, 1989.   25 p.   (Serie de bibliografías ocasionales, 17A)

> Updates an 1986 compilation with the same title.. It is an unannotated listing of works written by and about the great Puerto Rican intellectual who was a native of Mayagüez. All items mentioned are owned by the library.

2.057.   Rivera de Vélez, Laura. "Bibliografía." **Mairena** 10 (Winter 1988): 157-63.

> This unannotated bibliography forms part of an issue dedicated to Manuel Joglar Cacho, a distinguished poet from Manatí, Puerto Rico. Arranged chronologically, it is divided into the following sections:

books of poetry by Joglar Cacho (nineteen); translations into English (one item); anthologies (two); about the author and his work (ninety-six). The latter section includes books, journal and newspaper articles and prologues.

2.058.　　　Rodríguez Ramos, Esther.　"Aproximación a una bibliografía: René Marqués."　**Sin Nombre**　10 (October-December 1979):　121-48; **Revista del Instituto de Cultura Puertorriqueña** 82 (January-March 1979): 33-47.

Probably the most complete bibliography yet published on one of Puerto Rico's most famous dramatists who also excelled in other genres. The compiler states that it is by no means an exhaustive work. With regard to works by Marqués, the compiler describes the first editions only, with few exceptions. References to works written by the author are arranged chronologically under genres: poetry (one citation); stories (seven items); published dramas (fourteen works); unpublished dramas (eight entries); essays (two items); articles (ninety-two entries); reviews (fourteen citations); novels (two entries); works written for the Department of Education (twenty-three); and anthologies (one only). These are followed by an alphabetical section of 293 signed works of criticism, including books, articles and theses. The final section of the bibliography is a chronologically arranged list of seventy-two unsigned newspaper articles and news items written on René Marqués.

2.059.　　　Rodríguez Torres, Carmelo.　"Bibliografía mínima de José De Diego Padró."　**Sin Nombre**　6 (January-March 1976): 63-66.

Lists works by/about author Diego Padró. The first part cites his works by genre: poetry (three); novels (six); essays (one); works in anthologies (five); and various articles (six). The second section cites forty-four works of criticism.

2.060.　　　Román, Elba I.　"Enrique A. Laguerre: bibliografía."　**Faro**　12 (May 1988): 35-52.

Part of an issue dedicated completely to the study of the famous author. This unannotated list is limited to works owned by the Library of the Aguadilla Regional College of the University of Puerto Rico. It is organized alphabetically in the following parts: books by he author; index to Laguerre's "Complete Works"; criticisms in books (thirty-six entries); criticisms in journals (twenty items); reference sources for biographical information (eight references); and audio-visual resources (two items). An appendix consists of a chronology of

Laguerre's life, as taken from María del Carmen Monserrat's **Enrique A. Laguerre y 'Los amos benévolos'**.

2.061.   Rosenbaum, Sidonia C. "Eugenio María de Hostos: bibliografía." **Revista Hispánica Moderna** 5 (October 1939): 319-23.

Offers a complete bibliography of works written by Hostos and a selective listing of major works written about him. Attempts to include works not described in **América y Hostos**, by the Comisión Pro Celebración del Centenario del Natalicio de Eugenio María de Hostos.

2.062.   Ruscalleda Bercedóniz, Isabel María. "Bibliografía de José Luis González. **Textos de/sobre José Luis González**. México: Centro de Investigaciones Lingüístico-literarias de la Universidad Veracruzana, Instituto de Investigaciones Humanísticas, 1979, pp. 35-47.

This work was originally published in the journal **Texto Crítico** 4 (January-March 1979). The section of works written by González is organized chronologically by genre. Material about the author and his work is described in a separate section.

2.063.   Tirado, Amílcar, Nélida Pérez and Angel Aponte. **Juan Antonio Corretjer (1905-1985)**. New York: Centro de Estudios Puertorrriqueños, Hunter College, City University of New York, 1986. 44 p.

Lists material by/about Corretjer which can be found in the Centro Library. A bilingual introduction provides biographical information on Corretjer.

2.064.   _____, _____ and Rina Benmayor. **Luisa Capetillo (1879-1922)**. New York: Centro de Estudios Puertorriqueños, Hunter College, City University of New York, n.d. 15 p.

Brief bibliography of material written by/about Luisa Capetillo, one of the island's first female labor leaders. Biographical information can be obtained in the introduction.

2.065.   Tirado, Amílcar and Nélida Pérez. **René Marqués (1919-1979)**. New York: Centro de Estudios Puertorriqueños, Hunter College, City University of New York, 1986. 39 p.

A biographical study preceds the unannotated bibliography of works written by/about this well-loved Puerto Rican author.

2.066.   Torres Tapia, Manuel. "Fernando Sierra Berdecía, vida y obra; bibliografía selectiva." San Juan, P.R.: Asamblea Legislativa, 1971, 18 p. (mimeographed)

Sierra Berdecía was an important political figure and author. A biographical sketch precedes the bibliography which is arranged under the following headings: biographical sketches, works by the author (arranged by genre), studies and commentaries on Sierra.

2.067.   Universidad de Puerto Rico. Colegio Universitario Tecnológico de Ponce. Biblioteca. **Pedro Albizu Campos: bibliografía**. Ponce, P.R.: 1987. 14 p.

An alphabetical listing of books, journal and newspaper articles, pamphlets, posters and miscellaneous material by or about Albizu, a native of Ponce. All items can be found in the library. Much of the material was obtained from a private collector. One of the most complete bibliographies available.

2.068.   Universidad del Sagrado Corazón. Biblioteca Madre María Teresa Guevara. "Bibliografía selectiva de escritos de y sobre el insigne patriota puertorriqueño, que se encuentran en la Colección Puertorriqueña." [Santurce, P.R.: 1986] 8 p. (mimeographed)

Sacred Heart University is one of the largest private universities in the San Juan area. This bibliography cites a selection of works by/about the great Eugenio María de Hostos. All items can be found in the library.

2.069.   Vargas Pérez, Ramón. **Bibliografía del Dr. Salvador Arana Soto**. San Sebastián, P.R.: 1984. 60 p.

Covering the years 1935 to 1983, this chronological bibliography describes works by and about a prolific Puerto Rican author. Following a short biography of Arana Soto, the entries are presented in several sections: books and pamphlets; articles in journals and newspapers (ten subtopics); short stories; and poetry. A short section of works about Arana Soto precedes the list of sources consulted.

2.070.   Ward, James H. "Bibliografía de Luis Palés Matos." **La Torre** 31 (January-June 1973): 221-30.

This unannotated list describes works written by Luis Palés Matos, one of Puerto Rico's most famous poets. Three major divisions can be

identified: anthologies, poems and prose. Critical studies on Palés
are not cited.

2.071.   Zacarías de Justiniano, Esthervinda, Rita M. Seda de Rodríguez
and Lourdes Rivera Cruz. **Francisco Arriví: bibliografía selectiva**.
Mayagüez, P.R.:   Universidad de Puerto Rico, Recinto Universitario de
Mayagüez, Biblioteca, 1986. 11 p. (Serie de bibliografías ocasionales, 15)

Selected works by/about Francisco Arriví are described in this unannotated list. Cites books, journals and newpaper articles. Arriví is
best known as a dramatist and critic.

ECONOMICS AND INDUSTRIAL DEVELOPMENT

2.072.   Andic, Fuat M. and Suphan Andic. "An Annotated Bibliography of
the Economy of Puerto Rico, 1954-1969." In **Handbook of Latin American
Studies**. Vol. 31: 574-87. Gainesville, Fla.: University of Florida, 1969.

In the introduction of this special article, the authors identify some
areas of economics that have not yet been analyzed systematically.
This is an important source for materials published within the time
period indicated in the title. Covers books, journal articles and some
government publications.

2.073.   _____ and _____. "An Annotated Bibliography on the
Economy of Puerto Rico, 1969-1972." In **Handbook of Latin American
Studies**. Vol. 35: 225-34. Gainesville, Fla.: University of Florida, 1973.

Updates the bibliography published in volume thirty-one. Unlike the
original, it includes a section of doctoral dissertations taken from
Enid Baa's **Theses on Caribbean Topics** (1.007). Approximately
forty entries.

2.074.   Caraballo, María Judith. **Bibliografía anotada sobre los
recursos humanos**. San Juan, P.R.: Oficina del Gobernador, Consejo Estatal
de Empleo y Adiestramiento, 1980. 31 p.

Although not limited to Puerto Rico, the bibliography emphasizes
material on human resources in Puerto Rico. It deals with education,
employment and unemployment, statistics, migration, productivity
and housing. A supplement of fourteen leaves, published in the same
year, follows the same organization and reflects new titles received
in the Office.

2.075.   Caribbean Commission.   "Select Bibliography of Trade
Publications with Special Reference to Caribbean Trade Statistics..." [Port-
of-Spain, Trinidad: Central Secretariat, 1954] 54 p. (mimeographed)

> Puerto Rico is included in this selective bibliography of published
> sources of statistical information dealing with the overseas trade of
> Caribbean countries. Region-wide materials are also included.
> Entries are arranged by country issuing the publications.

2.076.   Caribbean Organization.   Library.   **Bibliography of
Development Plans.   Bibliographie des Plans de Developpment.**
Hato Rey, P.R.: Central Secretariat,1965. 9p.

> Arranged alphabetically by country, this bibliography includes
> twenty-two development plans for Puerto Rico. All plans described in
> the list can be found in the Library.

2.077.   Colegio Universitario de Cayey.   Biblioteca.   **Bibliografía
sobre el establecimiento de un superpuerto en Puerto Rico y
materias relacionadas.** Rev. ed. Cayey, P.R.: 1974. 35 p.

> The preparation of this bibliography was motivated by a controversy
> which arose as to the desireability and probability of constructing a
> superport in Puerto Rico. Entries are grouped under type of materials:
> government documents; miscellaneous reports and articles; news-
> paper articles, arranged by specific newspapers; recordings; and
> journal articles. Within each category the arrangement is chrono-
> logical. Symbols indicate libraries where each item may be found.

2.078.   Harvard University. Bureau for Economic Research in Latin
America. **The Economic Literature of Latin America: A Tentative
Bibliography.** 2 vols. Cambridge, Mass.: Harvard University Press, 1935-
36.

> Volume two includes a chapter on different aspects of Puerto Rico's
> economy (pages 215-30). Approximately 353 references are arranged
> under various subtopics. Author index.

2.079.   Hazlewood, Arthur. **The Economics of Under-Developed
Areas: An Annotated Reading List of Books, Articles and Official
Publications.** London, England: Oxford University Press, 1955. 89 p.

> This bibliography of English-language materials published between
> 1930 and 1953 includes references to Puerto Rico. They can be
> found by consulting the index of places.

2.080.   López, María Isabel. **Bibliografía del desarrollo económico e industrial de Puerto Rico, 1950-1975.** San Juan, P.R.: Administración de Fomento Económico, Oficina de Economía y Planificación, Biblioteca, 1975. 67 p. **Suplemento 1.** 1976. 20 p.

> Updates a previous bibliography which covered from 1950 to 1968 and was published in 1970. Consists of three sections: general concepts for the study of Puerto Rico's economic and industrial development; manufacturing ; and tourism. Includes unpublished studies and theses, as well as books and journal articles. Unannotated.

2.081.   Morris, James O. and Efrén Córdova. **Bibliography of Industrial Relations in Latin America.** Ithaca, N.Y.: New York State School of Industrial and Labor Relations, Cornell University, 1967. 290p.

> "The objective [of this bibliography] is to cover the literature bearing on the worker and the work relationship in all sectors of the economy...with or without unions, and regardless of employment, un-employment, or retirement status." Pages 262 to 270 cover Puerto Rico. Entries for books, dissertations, articles and some pamphlets are arranged alphabetically under subtopics. No annotations given.

2.082.   Puerto Rico. Administración de Fomento Económico. Oficina de Estudios Económicos. "Studies and Papers Prepared by the Office of Economic Research." San Juan, P.R.: The Administration, 1971. 54 p. (mimeographed)

> A subject-arranged list of studies prepared for the Office. Infor-mation given includes the title of the study or paper, its author(s) and the date.

2.083.   Sáenz Estades, Mercedes. **El desarrollo económico de PR a través de una bibliografía anotada, 1970-1975.** San Juan, P.R.: Comité Interagencial de la Estrategia, Consejo Financiero del Gobernador, 1975. 66 p.

> An annotated bibliography of theses and investigations carried out at the University of Puerto Rico during the period indicated in the title. It is organized alphabetically under the following topics: public administration; economic aspects of agriculture; science and tech-nology; commerce; communication; contamination control; economics; education; customs; income investment; economic planning; urban planning; population; material resources; superport; transportation; and tourism. A revised edition would be very useful.

2.084.   University of Wisconsin-Madison. Land Tenure Center Library.
Agrarian Reform in Latin America: An Annotated Bibliography. 2
vols. Madison, Wis.: University of Wisconsin, 1974.

> Nineteen references are given for agrarian reform in Puerto Rico.
> Four of them are identified as being of particular importance. Author
> and subject indexes included.

2.085.   Velázquez Gutiérrez, Andrés. **Compendio descriptivo de
fuentes de información sobre recursos humanos en Puerto Rico.**
San Juan, P.R.:   Oficina del Gobernador, Consejo Estatal de Empleo y
Adiestramiento, 1980. 52 p.

> Velázquez identifies sources of socio-economic information on the
> island's human resources. In addition to the list of sources, complete
> bibliographical information is given for each reference. under three
> major subject categories (preparation of human resources and census,
> data on human resources, data on population structure and dynamics).
> In addition, frequency, format, geographic area, contact person and a
> description of the content are also detailed.

2.086.   Velázquez Martín, E. "Budgeting Bibliography." Río Piedras, P.R.:
School of Public Administration, University of Puerto Rico, 1952. 83 p.
(mimeographed)

> This general bibliography on budgeting has a chapter on Puerto Rico.
> It appears to be a paper prepared as part of a class taken by the
> author. No indexes are provided.

2.087.   Weaver, Jerry L. **The Political Dimensions of Rural
Development in Latin America: A Selected Bibliography (1950–
1967).** Long Beach, Calif.: California State College, 1968; Santa Barbara,
Calif.: ABC-Clio, 1969. 87 p.

> This geographically arranged source includes references to over
> thirty-seven books, theses and articles on the political, economic and
> social development ofPuerto Rico. No annotations are given. Subject
> index. The 1969 version is entitled **Latin American Development:
> A Selected Bibliography (1950-1967).**

2.088.   Wilkinson, Andine. **The Caribbean Sugar Industry: A
Select Bibliography.** Cave Hill, Barbados: Institute of Social and
Economic Research (Eastern Caribbean), University of the West Indies, 1976.
87 p.

In addition to a general section, the bibliography has specific sections for each country, including Puerto Rico. Approximately thirty-two references describe different aspects of the sugar industry in Puerto Rico. Includes abbreviation symbols for libraries holding a copy of each item.

2.089.   Wish, John R. **Economic Development in Latin America :** **An Annotated Bibliography.** New York: Praeger, 1965. 144 p.

Emphasizes economic development, marketing, agriculture and communications. Access to the many references relating to Puerto Rico is made difficult by the lack of an index by country or a detailed subject index. Only an author index is provided.

EDUCATION

2.090.   Bulnes Aldunate, José María and Julio Torres. **Puerto Rico-** **UPR; Abrahán Díaz González, 1966-1969.** Cuernavaca, México: Centro Intercultural de Documentación, 1971. various pagings (CIDOC Dossier 29)

Describes 274 items relating to Chancellor Díaz during the years indicated with emphasis on the ROTC controversy (see 2.091). Arrangement appears to be roughly chronological.

2.091.   Bulnes Aldunate, José María and Julio Torres. **Puerto Rico-** **UPR; Reserve Officers Training Corps (ROTC).** Cuernavaca, México: Centro Intercultural de Documentación, 1971. 64 p. (CIDOC Dossier, 27)

Covering the presence of the ROTC on the Río Piedras campus and the unrest on campus from 1966 to 1969, this bibliography is divided into the following sections: leaflets, bulletins, student magazines; Academic Senate sessions, letters and official communiques re-arding modifications to ROTC courses; documents and press reactions relating to May 4, 1967; samples of the press for February 1968 to July 1969; daily newspaper articles, October 1969; daily newspaper articles, November 1969; position statements presented before the Academic Senate regarding the ROTC program; Student Council documents, 1969-1970; posters and hand bills on the March 1970 referendum; press reaction to March 4, police intervention on campus, murder of the student Antonia Martínez, referendum and graduation 1970. A helpful guide to a complex topic.

2.092.   Caribbean Commission.   Commission   des Caraibes.   **A** **Bibliography of Education in the Caribbean.   Bibliographie de**

l'enseignement dans la Caraibe. Compiled by V.O. Alcalá. Trinidad,
West Indies: Central Secretariat, 1959. 144 p.

> Covers education in the Caribbean countries of France, Great Britain,
> the Netherlands and the United States. The three main divisions of
> the work are: general education; instructional material; and
> educational serials. Author and subject indexes facilitate access to
> the materials which have been organized in chronological order under
> each country or area. "The great majority of the books dealing with
> Puerto Rican education are available in the Carnegie Library, San Juan,
> Puerto Rico."

2.093.   Corro, Alejandro del. **Puerto Rico: reforma universitaria
1963-65**. Cuernavaca, México: Centro Intercultural de Documentación,
1966. 1 vol. various pagings (CIDOC Dossier, 6)

> Information on university reform in Puerto Rico between 1963 and
> 1965 is referenced in three sections: official documents of the
> legislative process; documents of the University of Puerto Rico and
> others relating to the preparation of the new University Law; articles
> from newspapers and magazines. Many of the documents cited in the
> bibliography are reproduced in whole ore in part in another section of
> the book.

2.094.   Delgado, Juan Manuel. "Bibliografía sobre la Universidad de
Puerto Rico." **La Torre** 26 (January-December 1978): 225-45.

> Covers general aspects of the University of Puerto Rico and works of
> historical value, that is, works of prime importance for the writing of
> the institution's history. Not included, therefore, are works dealing
> exclusively with the regional colleges, schools, faculties, depart-
> ments and other dependencies. Articles from the university's journal
> **La Torre** are cited separately. Approximately 258 references are
> given.

2.095.   González Vélez, Isaura, Esthervinda Zacarías de Justiniano, and
Rita M. Seda de Rodríguez. **Historia del Recinto Universitario de
Mayagüez: bibliografía selectiva**. Mayagüez, P.R.: Universidad de
Puerto Rico, Recinto Universitario de Mayagüez, Biblioteca, 1986. 17 p.
(Serie de bibliografías ocasionales, 14)

> Entries are grouped by format. This unannotated bibliography aims to
> provide sufficient references to allow for the study of the campus's
> history since its founding in 1911.

2.096.   Lauerhass, Ludwig Jr. and Vera Lucía Oliveira de Araújo Haugse. **Education in Latin America: A Bibliography**. Los Angeles, Calif.: UCLA Latin American Center Publications, University of California; Boston: G. K. Hall, 1980. 431 p.

> "This bibliography is designed as an introductory reference volume for research on education in Latin America in all its formal and non-formal aspects from its beginning in pre-Columbian times to the mid-1970s..." The section on Puerto Rico (pages 138 to 146) is arranged by the following topics: serials and reference sources; education in general; in-school education; out-of-school education and special programs; and educational planning and administration.

2.097.   López Yustos, Alfonso. "Puerto Rico in the Field of Education: A Bibliography of Doctoral Research Studies." **Revista/Review Interamericana** 2 (Summer 1972): 158-66.

> Doctoral dissertations on education in Puerto Rico are described in alphabetical order under each of the following sections: general; administration and supervision; adult and community education; education of Puerto Ricans in New York City; elementary education; health education; higher education; history of education; language education; secondary education; teacher education and related studies. Unfortunately no annotations are given.

2.098.   Martínez, Magdalena. **Bibliografía de educación en Puerto Rico**. San Germán, P.R.: Universidad Interamericana de Puerto Rico, Recinto de San Germán, Biblioteca, Sala de Puerto Rico, 1980. 34 p.

> Describes books and journal articles from 1951 to 1978 as well as theses. Each section is divided by subtopics. All items are owned by the library.

2.099.   Morales de González, Emma. "Recursos bibliotecarios para investigación en el área de educación en Puerto Rico." In **Los recursos bibliotecarios para la investigación en el Caribe: documentos oficiales**, edited by Conferencia Anual de ACURIL (3rd: 1971: Caracas, Venezuela), 133-41. San Juan, P.R.: Asociación de Bibliotecas Universitarias y de Investigación del Caribe, 1978.

> An introductory essay describes publications and library collections dealing with Puerto Rico. It is followed by an unannotated bibliography.

2.100.   Ordoñez de Totis, María Elisa. **Bibliografía de la huelga universitaria de 1981**. Río Piedras, P.R.: Biblioteca José M. Lázaro, Biblioteca y Hemeroteca Puertorriqueña, 1982. 85 p.

> An unannotated bibliography on the student strike which took place from August 1981 through February of 1982. Material is divided by type of publication, then chronologically.

2.101.   Ortiz Guerra, Miguel Angel. **Bibliografía selectiva sobre educación en Puerto Rico; preparada en ocasión de celebrarse en el Recinto Universitario de Mayagüez un panel sobre reforma educativa**. Mayagüez, P.R.: Universidad de Puerto Rico, Recinto Universitario de Mayagüez, División de Extensión y Servicios a la Comunidad, 1986. 86 p.

> Entries are organized alphabetically under subtopics in three major chronological divisions: 1930 to 1955, 1955 to 1960, and 1960 to date. No annotations or index.

2.102.   Parker, Franklin and Betty June Parker. **Education in Puerto Rico and of Puerto Ricans in the U.S.A.; Abstracts of American Doctoral Dissertations**. San Juan, P.R.: Inter American University Press, 1978. 601 p.

> Lengthy abstracts accompany citations to 284 doctoral dissertations presented at American universities, whose subject was the education of Puerto Ricans on the island or on the mainland. A subject index adds to the usefulness of this work.

2.103.   Poston, Susan L. **Nonformal Education in Latin America: An Annotated Bibliography**. Los Angeles, Calif.: UCLA Latin American Center Publications, University of California, 1976. 268 p.

> The chapter on Puerto Rico (pages 179 to 184) deals with the following aspects of nonformal education: multifaceted programs; agricultural training; basic education/literacy; cooperative education; cultural extension; health, hygiene, and nutrition instruction; professional/paraprofessional training; vocational skills training; miscellaneous conceptualization.

2.104.   Puerto Rico. Consejo de Educación Superior. Oficina de Asesoramiento Financiero. "Bibliografía sobre la educación en Puerto Rico." Río Piedras, P.R.: n.d. 7 p. (mimeographed)

Approximately 114 references to education in Puerto Rico are given in random order. Some entries lack complete bibliographic information. Should be revised and updated.

2.105.   Puerto Rico. Departamento de Instrucción Pública. **Indice de libros en circulación.** San Juan, P.R.: 1955? 133 p.

Lists useful books available for teachers. Grade level is indicated as well as full bibliographic information. Arranged by subjects, the book lacks author and title indexes. Also of historical interest.

2.106.   _____. _____ **Indice de publicaciones para uso en las escuelas públicas.** San Juan, P.R.: 1966. 266 p.

Cites useful books for public school teachers. Suggested grade levels are indicated. Both general and Puerto Rican titles are covered by this subject-arranged listing. No indexes.

2.107.   _____. _____ Pública.. **Bibliografía.** San Juan, P.R.: Departamento de Instrucción Pública, Centro de Recursos e Investigaciones Pedagógicas, 1972-

The bibliography describes the Center's holdings. Many entries deal specifically with education in Puerto Rico. Only the first two issues of the first volume were found and examined. The subjects covered in each one varied.

2.108.   Universidad de Puerto Rico.   Centro de Investigaciones Pedagógicas. **Bibliografía anotada de preescolares.** Prepared by Jennie Rivera and others. Río Piedras, P.R.: 1972. 67 p.

The first part of this bibliography cites books, reports and journal and newspaper articles published on the island in the 1960s and dealing with the topic of preschoolers (pages 1 to 14). The second part includes general material published elsewhere.

2.109.   _____. _____. **Indice bibliográfico de investigaciones pedagógicas, 1948-1968.** 2 vols. in 4 Río Piedras, P.R.: Universidad de Puerto Rico, Recinto de Río Piedras, 1976. (833 p.)

About 1,375 studies are cited in this bibliography on education in Puerto Rico. It includes works done in other countries as well as studies made on the island. Volume one, published in three parts, covers masters and doctoral theses and other investigations. It is arranged by subject and has an author index. Annotations or summaries are provided for most entries. Volume two includes journal articles, conference proceedings or presentations, annual reports, laws and other government or university publications. It is also arranged by subject with an author index.

2.110.   Universidad de Puerto Rico. Facultad de Pedagogía. Biblioteca Sellés. "Bibliografía de tésis y monografías presentadas en el Depto. de Estudios Graduados de la Facultad de Pedagogía, Universidad de Puerto Rico, Recinto de Río Piedras, 1966-76." Río Piedras, P.R.: 1977. 47, 57 p. (mimeographed)

Two main sections make up the body of the work: authors and subjects. Many of the items cited deal with education in Puerto Rico.

2.111.   Universidad Interamericana de Puerto Rico, San Germán. "Indice de artículos sobre educación en lengua española. Spanish Language Education Index I.A.U." [San Germán, P.R.: 1972?] 30 p. (mimeographed)

A subject index to articles on education found in 40 Spanish-language journals. Numerous references to education in Puerto Rico are included. Covers 1969 to 1972 only. An updated version would prove most useful.

FOLKLORE

2.112.   Boggs, Ralph Steele. **Bibliography of Latin American Folklore: Tales, Festivals, Customs, Arts, Magic, Music.** New York: H. W. Wilson, 1940; Detroit: Blaine Ethridge, 1971. 109 p. (Inter-American Bibliographical and Library Association Publications, Series I, vol.5)

Each topic is subdivided geographically. There are seventeen specific references to Puerto Rican folklore.

2.113.   Harrison, Ira E. and Sheila Cosminsky. **Traditional Medicine, Ethnopharmacology, Maternal and Child Health, Mental Health and Public Health; An Annotated Bibliography of Africa, Latin America, and the Caribbean.** New York: Garland Publishing, 1976. 229 p.

A "survey of the salient literature on the topic of traditional medicine written after World War II, from 1950-1975. By traditional medicine, we mean native medical systems (healers, therapies and beliefs)... [that] do not depend upon western technology." Includes twelve references to Puerto Rico and Puerto Ricans living on the mainland.

2.114.   Marcano Zorilla, Enriqueta. "Bibliografía para el estudio de la imaginaría popular puertorriqueña." **Revista del Instituto de Cultura Puertorriqueña** 14 (July-September 1971): 52-56.

> Carvings of saints ("santos") are an important part of Puerto Rico's folklore and art. This bibliography of the subject is divided by books, journals and newspaper articles. The latter section is arranged by newspaper, then chronologically under each. A small section of other sources includes audiovisual materials, exhibition catalogs, etc. The bibliography concludes with a list of important collections.

GEOGRAPHY AND HISTORY

2.115.   Beers, Henry Putney. **Bibliographies in American History, 1942-1978:   Guide to Materials for Research**. 2 vols. Woodbridge, Conn.: Research Publications, 1982. 946 p.

> Treats history in its widest sense and covers both North and South America. Listings for Puerto Rican bibliographies can be found in volume two. Beers gives bibliographic data for thirty well-chosen bibliographies.

2.116.   **Bibliografía   americanista   española,   1935-1963.** Seville, Spain: Comité Organizador del XXXVI Congreso Internacional de Americanistas, 1964. 565 p.

> Attempts to include all books and periodicals published within the time span indicated. The major divisions of the work are: general works, anthropology, modern America and contemporary Latin America. More than forty of the 5,460 entries refer to Puerto Rico.

2.117.   "Bibliografía esclavista." **Indice**, 13 March 1930, p. 194.

> Mentions thirty-seven items related to slavery in Puerto Rico. No annotations or introduction are given. **Indice** was a highly respected literary and cultural magazine.

2.118.   Caro Costas, Aida, Catalina Palerm and Luis de la Rosa. "Informe de la labor de investigación realizada en los archivos de la ciudad de Santo Domingo." **Boletín de la Academia Puertorriqueña de la Historia** 6 (January 1975): 115-45.

> Provides a description of historical documents and other materials found in different archives, libraries and private collections in the

Dominican Republic. Its usefulness lies in the descriptions of documents relating to Puerto Rico and in the identification of those collections which do **not** have any relevant materials. Important items dealing with the nationalist movement are also described. This should prove a useful aid to researchers.

2.119.   Castro, María de los Angeles. "Guía descriptiva de los fodos documentales existentes en el Centro de Investigaciones Históricas." **Cuadernos de la Facultad** (Universidad de Puerto Rico) 10 (1983): 89-115.

An introduction explains the purpose of the Center as well as the sources and importance of its resources. These materials are then listed and described under the following categories: microfilm collection (documents and print materials); microfiche collection; collection of photocopies, photographs and manuscript or typewritten copies (by country of origin); private collections; original documents; collection of transcribed documents; collection of articles and monographs; supplementary resources for research; taped conferences; books and journals; and theses. This article was also published as part of the first edition of **Los primeros pasos** (1984) but did not appear in the second edition.

2.120.   _____. "The Historical Archives of Puerto Rico." In **Latin American Masses and Minorities: Their Images and Realities,** edited by Seminar on the Acquisition of Latin American Library Materials (30th: 1985: Princeton, N.J.), vol.2: 573-79. Madison, Wisc.: SALALM Secretariat, 1987.

Describes collections and publications under the following headings: general guides; archives and major libraries; private archives; and personal collections. Partially annotated.

2.121.   _____, María Dolores Luque and Gervasio Luis García. **Los primeros pasos; una bibliografía para empezar a investigar la historia de Puerto Rico**. 2d rev. ed. Río Piedras, P.R.: Ediciones Huracán, 1987. 130 p.

This is the most complete bibliographic guide for the study of Puerto Rican history yet published. Although the book is unannotated, each chapter begins with an introduction. The first chapter lists general works on historical theory and methodology. The remaining chapters deal with Puerto Rican sources as follows: archives and libraries; bibliographies, historiography and criticism; document collections; law; dictionaries and encyclopedias; chronicles; secondary sources (by topic); the metropolis (that is, Spain, United States and Africa); comparative history; and journals. This is a revised and updated edition of the original work published by the University of Puerto Rico in 1984. The original edition also contained Castro's guide to the documents housed in the Center for Historical Research (see 2.119).

2.122.   Castro, María de los Angeles, María Dolores Luque de Sánchez and Gervasio Luis García. **Los primeros pasos: una bibliografía para empezar a investigar la historia de Puerto Rico. Guía descriptiva de los fondos documentales existentes en el Centro de Investigaciones Históricas,** by María de los Angeles Castro. Río Piedras, P.R.: Centro de Investigaciones Hisóricas, Oficina de Publicaciones, Facultad de Humanidades, 1984. 111 p.

This first edition of **Los primeros pasos** lacks much of the infor-mation that can be found in the second (2.121). However, it includes a copy of one of Castro's articles previously published (2.119)

2.123.   **A Catalogue of Maps of Hispanic America, including Maps in Scientific Periodicals and Books and Sheet and Atlas Maps with Articles on the Cartography of the Several Countries and Maps Showing the Extent and Character of Existing Surveys.** 4 vols. New York: American Geographic Society, 1930.

The section on the West Indies in the first volume includes many ref-erences to Puerto Rico. Unfortunately the index does not pinpoint ref-erences to specific coutnries, and as a result one must read each entry to determine the country studied.

2.124.   Cibes Viadé, Alberto. **Guión temático y bibliografía (Historia de Puerto Rico).** Río Piedras, P.R.: Editorial Edil, 1978. 64 p.

The first part of this guide is a chronologically organized outline of topics in Puerto Rican history. The second part is a selective bibliography of primary and secondary materials.   Unfortunately, complete bibliographical information is not supplied. For books, only author and title are indicated, while the information supplied for periodical references varies greatly.

2.125.   Davidson, William V. **Geographical Research on Latin America: A Cartographic Guide and Bibliography of Theses and Dissertations, 1909-1978.** N.p.: 1980. 52 p.

"Prepared for the Tenth Anniversary Meeting Conference of Latin Americanist Geographers, Muncie, Indiana, April 1980." Describes

over 800 masters and doctoral theses on Latin American geography.
Besides listing general studies on Latin America, the bibliography
describes, in chronological order, forty-two theses dealing with the
geography of Puerto Rico. Most are doctoral dissertations.

2.126.   Donoso, Ricardo. **Fuentes documentales para la historia
de la independencia de América.** Mexico: Comisión de Historia del
Instituto Panamericano de Geografía e Historia, 1968-

This is an inventory of archival material on the independence movement in Latin America. The first volume has eighteen references to
Puerto Rico. A description of each document or collection accompanies each entry. The book is organized by archive.

2.127.   Fernández Méndez, Eugenio. **The Sources on Puerto Rican
Culture History: A Critical Appraisal.** San Juan, P.R.: Ediciones "El
Cemí", 1967. 55 p.

An authoritative, extended bibliographic essay on sources for the
study of Puerto Rico's history. Three main groups of sources are
studied: basic documentary sources ; narratives or chronicles; and
material "written by Puerto Rican historians or foreigners that bear a
particularly intimate knowledge of the local situation." Includes a
description of the different archives that may be consulted for
historical research. No index.

2.128.   Gandía Córdova, Ramón. "Datos históricos del estudio de la
geografía de Puerto Rico." **Revista de Obras Públicas** 5 (January 1928):
1485-87.

This bibliographic essay describes books, atlases and miscellaneous
publications related to the geography of Puerto Rico from the
sixteenth to the twentieth centuries.

2.129.   González Ginorio, José. **El descubrimiento de Puerto Rico:
suplemento bibliográfico.** San Juan, P.R.: 1938. 69 p.

Published as a supplement to the original work of the same title.
Lengthy commentaries accompany this chronological description of
materials dealing with Christopher Colombus's second voyage to the
New World. It also fills in omissions discovered in the original work.
A reprint edition was published in 1971 by Editorial Coquí.

2.130.   Griffin, Charles C, ed. **Latin America: A Guide to the Historical Literature**. Austin, Tex.: University of Texas Press, 1971. 700 p.
> Very selective bibliography covering materials published to 1966. The arrangement is basically chronological. Sections on Puerto Rico can be located by consulting the table of contents and the index. General sections on the Caribbean may also be considered.

2.131.   **Guía de fuentes para la historia de Ibero-America conservadas en España**. 2 vols. Madrid, Spain: Dirección General de Archivos y Bibliotecas, 1966-69.

> Although this work covers up to 1914, the Puerto Rican section only includes documents to 1898, the year in which the United States gained control of the island during the Spanish American War. Items in volume one describe material from historical archives, public administration, military and ecclesiastical archives in Spain. The second volume cites documents from private archives, libraries and cultural institutions. Entries give brief descriptions of the documents or materials. Helpful indexes by place, name and subject add to the value of the work.

2.132.   Hogg, Peter C. **The African Slave Trade and its Suppression: A Classified and Annotated Bibliography of Books, Pamphlets and Periodical Articles**. London: Frank Cass, 1973. 409 p.

> This subject bibliography includes thirteen references to Puerto Rico, as found in the geographic name index. Most of the items described are lesser-known titles. Therefore, the investigator should consult other bibliographies for more complete and authoritative references.

2.133.   Instituto de Cultura Puertorriqueña. Archivo General de Puerto Rico. **Guía al Archivo General de Puerto Rico**. San Juan, P.R.: 1964. 167p.

> In this bibliography of material housed in the General Archives of Puerto Rico, entries are arranged alphabetically by government agency. A brief description is given of each item included, as well as the subject treated, the quantity of documents and their arrangement, and the size and condition of the document or collection.

2.134.   Martínez de Hernández, Tomasita. **Culturas precolombinas de Puerto Rico: los igneri, los taínos, los caribes; bibliografía selectiva**. Mayagüez, P.R.:   Universidad de Puerto Rico, Recinto

Universitario de Mayagüez, Biblioteca, 1985. 30 p. (Serie de bibliografías ocasionales, 10)

A useful compilation of material dealing with the Precolumbian cultures of Puerto Rico. The first two sections (books and journal articles) are arranged alphabetically while the third section (newspaper articles and pamphlets) is organized by subjects. Unannotated.

2.135.   Mason, Lois E. **Bibliography of Latin America: 1955-1964; Books, Monographs, Periodicals, Articles.** Columbus, Ohio: Department of Geography, Ohio State University, 1965. 23 p.

The Puerto Rican section includes references to works of general and physical geography, oceanography, meteorology, economy, trade, agriculture, urban geography, industry and minerals and fuels. Twenty-nine items are listed.

2.136.   Monteiro, Palmyra V. M. **A Catalogue of Latin American Flat Maps, 1926-1964.** 2 vols. Austin, Tex.: Institute of Latin American Studies, The University of Texas at Austin, 1967.

Volume one includes a section on general and topic flat maps of Puerto Rico. It does not cover maps in books and periodicals. Almost all maps described were published by government agencies at different levels.

2.137.   Morales Padrón, Francisco, J. Gil-Bermejo and María Teresa Garrido. "Cartografía sobre Puerto Rico en París, Londres y Madrid." **Anuario de Estudios Americanos** 18 (1961): 615-49.

One hundred fifteen maps and plans are described in this work which is organized by collection: Bibliothèque National (Paris), the British Museum (London), Royal Department of the Admiralty (London), and Museo Naval (Madrid). Each entry includes a physical description, size and number assigned, where applicable.

2.138.   New York Public Library. Map Division. **Catalog of the Map Division.** 10 vols. Boston: G. K. Hall, 1971.

Reproduces library cards for maps, atlases and other cartographic publications. Approximately seventy entries refer to Puerto Rican maps and materials.

2.139.   Ortega Benayas, María Angeles and María Teresa Díez de los Ríos San Juan. **Inventario de la serie 'Oficios de Guerra' de Puerto Rico.**

Under the direction of María Teresa de la Peña Marazuela. Madrid, Spain: Ministerio de Cultura, 1980. 457 p. (Archivo Histórico Nacional. Sección de Ultramar, 5)

> A chronological bibliography of primary material covering military communications and orders from 1836 to 1893. Also a good source of biographical information on military personnel. Includes onomastic, geographic and subject indexes.

2.140.   Peña y De la Cámara, José María de la. **A List of Spanish "Residencias" in the Archives of the Indies, 1516-1775: Administrative Judicial Reviews of Colonial Officials in the American Indies, Philippine and Canary Islands.** Washington, D.C.: Library of Congress, Reference Department, 1955. 109 p.

> This bibliography describes documents on judicial reviews ("residencias") of Spanish offficials which are housed in the Archives of the Indies. They are grouped in two sections: "justicia" series where Puerto Rico falls under the Audiencia de Santo Domingo, 1516-76; and the "Escribanía de la Cámara" series where Puerto Rico is dealt with separately (pages 21-22). The place and name index includes references to Puerto Rico and to individual officials.

2.141.   Peña Marazuela, María Teresa de la . **Inventario de la serie de hacienda de Puerto Rico.** With the collaboration of María Teresa Diez de los Ríos y María Angeles Ortega Benayas. Madrid, Spain: Ministerio de Cultura, 1979. 796 p. (Archivo Histórico Nacional. Sección de Ultramar, 4)

> Important bibliography of the administration of the island's economy and finances in the nineteenth century. Arranged alphabetically by subject in each of three chronological periods: from the beginning of the century to1850; 1851 to 1875; 1876 to 1899. An introductory essay explains the arrangement of the book as well as discussing the office of the intendent (lists the people who occupied the position), the monetary problem, and additional archival collections that could help the researcher. Excellent and useful indexes of names, geographic locations and subjects.

2.142.   _____. **Inventario de la serie fomento de Puerto Rico.** Madrid, Spain: Servicio de Educación y Ciencia, 1972.   224 p. (Archivo Histórico Nacional. Sección de Ultramar, 2)

> This is a useful bibliography of archival material relating to the Spanish government's administration of agriculture, commerce,

industry, education and public works in nineteenth century Puerto
Rico. Excellent indexes facilitate the use of this source.

2.143.   Peña Marazuela, María Teresa de la. **Inventario de la serie
gobierno de Puerto Rico.** With the collaboration of José Ramón Barraca
Ramos, Isabel Echávarri Lomo y M. Angeles Ortega Benayas. Madrid, Spain:
Servicio de Publicaciones del Ministerio de Educación y Ciencia, 1972? 224
p. (Archivo Histórico Nacional. Sección de Ultramar, I)

Exhaustive bibliography of primary material housed in Spain's
National Archives, Overseas Section, relating to the government and
administration of Puerto Rico in the nineteenth century. Onomastic,
geographic and subject indexes facilitate access to the documents.
Includes an index to persons with separatist ideas as well as a brief
description of other Spanish archives and offices where more
documents can be found relating to the island.

2.144.   _____ **Inventario de la serie gracia y justicia de
Puerto Rico.** With the collaboration of María José Arranz Recio and María
Angeles Ortega Benayas. Madrid, Spain: Servicio de Publicaciones del
Ministerio de Educación y Ciencia, 1975. 354 p. (Archivo Histórico Nacional.
Sección de Ultramar, 3)

Cites primary sources which are useful for the study of nineteenth
century Spanish judicial institutions in Puerto Rico, lawyers and
"procuradores" as well as ecclesiastical questions. The latter are
included here since the Spanish crown, as patron of the Indies, had to
approve construction of all church buildings as well as the appoint-
ments of all bishops and archbishops. The onomastic, geographical
and topical indexes are indispensable for the effective use of this
publication.

2.145.   Picó, Fernando. "Fuentes para la historia de las comunidades
rurales en Puerto Rico en los siglos 19 y 20." In **Latin American Masses
and Minorities: Their Images and Realities,** edited by Seminar on the
Acquisition of Latin American Library Materials (30th: 1985: Princeton,
N.J.), vol. 1: 255-78. Madison, Wisc.: SALALM Secretariat, 1987.

One of Puerto Rico's most distinguished contemporary historians
draws upon personal experience for this bibliographic essay on the
strengths and weaknesses of available sources for the study of the
history of rural island communities. It was subsequently published in
Spanish as "Fuentes para la historia de las comunidades rurales en
Puerto Rico durante los siglos 19 y 20" in **Op. Cit.: Boletín del
Centro de Investigaciones Históricas** (U.P.R.), on pages 1 to 13 of

the first issue (1985-1986).

2.146.   Rodríguez Cruz, Juan. "Documentos sobre Puerto Rico que se encuentran en los Archivos Nacionales de los Estados Unidos (R.G.   186)." **Caribbean Studies** 5 (October 1965): 32-50.

Describes a selection of documents housed in the National Archives. Rodríguez organizes the materials in seven groups: political and civil affairs, 1754-1897; fiscal matters, 1782-1896; military matters, 1761-1890; naval affairs, 1782-1891; ecclesiastical matters, 1782-897; documents originating in different government agencies, 1796-1897; municipal documents. Of the latter group, items dealing with Mayagüez are described as illustrative of materials to be found on the towns of Puerto Rico.

2.147.   Rodríguez Villafañe, Leonardo. **Catálogo de mapas y planos de Puerto Rico en el Archivo General de Indias.** San Juan, P.R.: Municipio de San Juan, 1966. 134 p.

Chronologically arranged, this list describes maps and plans of Puerto Rico that can be found in the General Archives of the Indies in Spain. Each entry includes a reproduction of the map or plan, a description, an indication of whether the item is in color or not, size in inches, location within the Archives, section of origin and any other relevant information. Topical, onomastic and geographic indexes are most helpful in locating specific types of documents.

2.148.   Roessingh, M. P. H. **Guide to the Sources in the Netherlands for the History of Latin America.** The Hague, Netherlands: Government Publishing Office, 1968. 232 p.

A bibliography of documents, manuscripts, maps and topographical reproductions in the archives and libraries of the Netherlands. Includes references to four collections containing material on Puerto Rico.

2.149.   Rosa Martínez, Luis de la. "Los fondos documentales en el Archivo General de Puerto Rico." **Anales de Investigación Histórica** (U.P.R.) 4 (1977): 1-20.

Describes some of the most useful series of documents in the General Archives of Puerto Rico for the study of municipal or micro-history. All documents date from the nineteenth century. They include: territorial court ("Audiencia Territorial"); provincial delegation ("Diputación Provincial"); intendency ("Intendencia"); notary protocols

("protocolos notariales"); public works; governors (documents re-
turned to Puerto Rico by the federal government in1973); and municipalities, except San Germán, Ponce, Mayagüez, Caguas and Vega Baja.

2.150.   Rosario Natal, Carmelo and Francisco Scarano Fiol.
"Bibliografía histórica puertorriqueña de la década de los setentas (1970-
1979)." **Homines** 6 (January-June 1982): 193-219. (Reprinted in
Homines 8 (January 1984): 83-109.)

The authors affirm that the 1970s saw an explosion in historical
interest in Puerto Rico. For that reason they prepared this unannotated bibliography of works written during the decade on the island's
history. Entries are arranged alphabetically under topics.

2.151.   Salinero, José. "Manuscritos sobre Puerto Rico en la Biblioteca
Nacional de Madrid." **Horizontes** 14 (April 1971): 61-94.

Physical and bibliographic descriptions are given for documents which
deal with Puerto Rico and can be found in the National Library of
Madrid. Arranged chronologically, entries also provide the number
assigned by the Library. Some commentaries on the usefulness or
importance of the documents are included.

2.152.   Santana, Arturo.   "Puerto Rico."   **Historiografía y
Bibliografía Americanista** (1957): 163-192.

This bibliographical essay describes principal historical literature
published from 1951 to 1957. The year 1951 was chosen because it
corresponded to the year in which the journal **Historia** began publication. It covers texts and sources, historiography, general studies
and monographs, prehistory, discovery and colonization, nineteenth
century, twentieth century, biographies (incorrectly labelled bibliographies) and literary and art history.

2.153.   Seville.   Instituto Hispano-Cubano de Historia de América.
**Catálogo de los fondos americanos del Archivo de Protocolos de
Sevilla**. Madrid, Spain: Compañía Ibero-Americana de Publicaciones, 1930-

A chronologically arranged bibliography of documents which may be of
interest for the study of the history of the Americas. Indexes by subject, persons and places provide for effective access to the materials
described in the entries. In a separte appendix are reproduced certain
documents considered to be of exceptional interest due to the persons
involved or to their state of conservation which permitted a good

2.154.   Silvestrini Pacheco, Blanca and María de los Angeles Castro. "Sources for the Study of Puerto Rican History: A Challenge to the Historian's Imagination." **Latin American Research Review** 16 (1981): 156-71.

> A bibliographical essay on primary sources available for the study of Puerto Rico's history. It also describes, in general terms, the municipal holdings and notarial records of the General Archives of Puerto Rico. Appendix one outlines documentary sources housed at the Puerto Rican collection of the University of Puerto Rico Library. Appendix two is a bibliography of documentary series related to Puerto Rico. Useful bibliographical information can also be found in the end notes.

2.155.   Spain.   Archivo General de Indias, Seville.   **Catálogo de documentos de la sección novena del Archivo General de Indias**. Vol. 1: Series 1 and 2: **Santo Domingo, Cuba, Puerto Rico, Luisiana, Florida y México**. Seville, Spain: Escuela de Estudios Hispánicos, 1949. 822 p.

> Arranged chronologically by series or audiences, this bibliogrphy describes documents housed in the ninth section of the General Archives of the Indies. Each entry includes the following elements: catalog number; date and place; abstract of the document and appendices or other added pages; total number of leaves and size; location folios code.The index has entries by topic, geographic location and proper names, thus providing access to documents of interest for the study of Puerto Rico.

2.156.   Tirado Merced, Dulce María.   "Colonialismo, revolución y reformismo: Puerto Rico en los archivos cubanos." **Cuadernos de la Facultad de Humanidades** (Universidad de Puerto Rico) 10 (1983): 71-87.

> Describes the contents and importance of copies of Cuban documents relating to Puerto Rico and housed in the Center's Library. The documents are divided into seven categories: miscellaneous records from 1777 to 1873; Puerto Rican section of the Cuban Revolutionary Party; Cuban Liberal Party; "Actas de Constitución" de la Sociedad Republicana de Cuba y Puerto Rico, 1865; articles from the newspaper **La revolución Cuba y Puerto Rico**, 1869-1871; 1887 as seen from Cuba; and Betances as seen by his contemporaries. The appendix gives more details on each section.

2.157.   Tudela de la Orden, José. **Los manuscritos de América en las bibliotecas de España.** Madrid: Ediciones Cultura Hispánica, 1954. 586 p.

Provides descriptions of manuscripts relating to America and housed in the public libraries of Spain. Although entries are arranged by public libraries, library or collection, access to items relating to Puerto Rico is assured by the inclusion of subject and geographic indexes. Also cited are several theses, such as María Cadilla's and Antonia Saez's.

2.158.   Ulibarri, George and John P. Harrison. **Guide to Materials on Latin America in the National Archives of the United States.** Washington, D.C.: National Archives and Records Service, General Services Administration, 1974. 489 p.

This selective bibliography of representative documents describes permanent non-current records. It is arranged similarly to the organization of the American government: by branch and then by department. Access to Puerto Rican materials is expedited by the inclusion of a general index of authors, subjects, countries, and municipalities. Thus the researcher may consult the index under "Puerto Rico", "Puerto Rican", and the name of a specific town or person. Records described usually "provide general information as to type, purpose, content, chronological span and quality."

2.159.   Uricoechea, Ezequiel. "Mapoteca   colombiana."   **Boletín Cultural y Bibliográfico** 5 (1962): 1480-88.

Forms part of a bibliogrphy of maps published in London in 1860 and reproduced in various issues of the **Boletín.** Pages 1486 and 1487 give details of eleven maps of Puerto Rico whose imprint dates range from 1785 to 1851. Other issues of the journal include references to general maps of Latin America and the Antilles.

2.160.   Vázquez Sotillo, Nelly. "Relación de mapas, planos y fotografías existentes en el Centro de Investigaciones Históricas." **Op. Cit.: Boletín del Centro de Investigaciones Históricas** (Universidad de Puerto Rico) 1 (1985-1986): 125-54.

Provides brief descriptions of materials (maps, plans and photographs) found in the above-mentioned Center. Entries are arranged chronologically under archive or collection.

2.161.   Velázquez Chávez, María del Carmen. **Guía bibliográfica de la historia en Hispano-América.** México: Instituto Panamericano de Geografía e Historia, Comisión de Historia, 1964. 506 p. (Bibliografías, 2. Publicaciones, no. 224)

> Included in this guide to Latin American history is a section of general references to Latin America followed by chapters on individual countries. Chapter twenty, which covers Puerto Rico (pages 427 to 434), is subdivided into general references, historiography, document collections, bibliography and serial publications. Approximately forty-eight citations refer to Puerto Rico. Some annotations are included.

2.162.   Vila Vilar, Enriqueta. "Bibliografía básica para la historia de Puerto Rico." **Historiografía y Bibliografía Americanista** 23 (1979): 97-116.

> This is an unprefaced, annotated bibliography of basic sources for the study of Puerto Rican history. Each of the following categories is organized alphabetically: general works; pre-Hispanic era; discovery and conquest; colonial period; nineteenth century; twentieth century; bibliographies; and serial publications of an historical nature. Approximately 156 entries. The compiler is also the author of a number of books on Puerto Rican history.

2.163.   Walne, Peter. **A Guide to Manuscript Sources for the History of Latin America and the Caribbean in the British Isles.** London, England: Oxford University Press, 1973. 580 p.

> This bibliography of public and private archival sources related to Latin American history contains a number of documents relevant to Puerto Rico. They can be found by consulting the index.

2.164.   Welch, Thomas L. and Myriam Figueras. **Travel Accounts and Descriptions of Latin America and the Caribbean, 1800-1920; A Selected Bibliography.** Washington, D.C.: Columbus Memorial Library, Organization of American States, 1982.   293 p.   (Documentation and Information Series, no. 6) (OEA/SG/O.1/IV/III.6)

> Puerto Rico appears on pages 216 to 219 of this geographically organized, selective bibliography. It cites English-language sources only, most posterior to 1898.

LANGUAGE AND LINGUISTICS

2.165.   Chatham, James R. and Enrique Ruiz-Fornells. **Dissertations Completed in the United States and Canada, 1876-1966.** With the collaboration of Sara Matthews Scales. Lexington, Ky.: The University Press of Kentucky, 1970. 120 p.

Dissertations are arranged by subject following the scheme used in **PMLA International Bibliography**, prior to June 1968. Key words in the titles were used in classifying entries. Where possibe, details are given for those dissertations which were later published. Although dissertations on teachingwere not covered, all other titles "of obvious interest to researchers in Hispanic languages and literatures" were described. The general index can be used to pinpoint items of interest to Puerto Rican studies by searching under "Puerto Rico", "Puerto Rican..." and names such as Hostos.

2.166.   _____ and Carmen C. McLendon. **Dissertations in Hispanic Languages and Literatures: An Index on Dissertations Completed in the United States and Canada.** With the collaboration of Enrique Ruiz-Fornells and Sara Matthews Scales. Lexington, Ky.: The University Press of Kentucky, 1981. 162 p.

Continues the previous title, covering 1967 to 1977. However, the arrangement is alphabetical by author. This edition describes 3,527 dissertations and includes indexes of Catalan language and literature, Luso-Brazilian language and literature and Spanish and Spanish American language and literature. It provides retrospective references to dissertations on the teaching and learning of Hispanic languages as well as bilingualism. Access to material relating to Puerto Rico is provided by the headings "Puerto Rican literature", "Puerto Rican Spanish", and "Puerto Rico" in the Spanish and Spanish American language and literature index.

2.167.   "El español en Puerto Rico: bibliografía ." **Revista de Estudios Hispánicos** (Puerto Rico) 1 (January-June 1971): 111-24.

No introduction explains the scope or purpose of this unannotated listing of 318 items. Books, articles, theses and conferences are included. A subject arrangement might have increased the work's usefulness since a wide range of subjects is covered: linguistics, school texts, teaching of Spanish, pronunciation, etymology, grammar and others.

2.168.   Nichols, Madeline W., ed. **A Bibliographical Guide to
Materials on American Spanish**. Cambridge, Mass.: Harvard University
Press, 1941. 114 p. (Committee on Latin American Studies. American
Council of Learned Societies. Miscellaneous publication, 2)

> An annotated bibliography on the Spanish language in the Americas.
> The section on Puerto Rico (pages 97 to 98) describes fifteen items
> under the following headings: general; dictionaries and vocabularies;
> individual words; toponymy; flora and fauna.

2.169.   Ocampo, Tarsicio. **Puerto Rico idioma escolar, 62-65:
reacciones de prensa**. Cuernavaca, México: Centro Intercultural de
Documentación, 1966. 260 p. (CIDOC Dossier, 1)

> A chronologically organized bibliography of 780 items dealing with a
> controversy on the language of instruction in Puerto Rico. The debate
> arose from a press conference given by the then Secretary of Instruc-
> tion, Cándido Oliveras, and lasted from June 1962 through 1966.
> Emphasis is on the press reaction to the debate. Many articles and
> documents are reproduced as well. Author index appended.

2.170.   Powers, Michael. "American Dissertations in Puerto Rican
Spanish and/or English Linguistics." **Revista de Estudios Hispánicos**
(Puerto Rico) 11 (1984): 215-17.

> Twenty-two dissertations are described. The introduction discusses
> the number of studies done on each of the fourteen subtopics. For
> each entry the author, thesis title, university and year are indicated.

2.171.   Reinecke, John E. **A Bibliography of Pidgin and Creole
Languages**. Honolulu: The University of Hawaii, 1975. 804 p. (Oceanic
Linguistics Special Publications, 14)

> Includes general references to pidgin and creole languages as well as
> eighteen specific references to language in Puerto Rico. Some anno-
> tations are given. Indexes.

2.172.   Rivas, Rafael Angel et al. **Bibliografía sobre el español del
Caribe hispánico**. Caracas, Venezuela: Instituto Universitario Pedagógico
de Caracas, 1985. 294 p.

> Attempts to list materials useful for the study of the Spanish spoken
> in the Caribbean region. Three major sections make up the work:
> bibliographies; general studies of Caribbean Spanish; and specific
> studies by country. Puerto Rico is included in the latter section on

pages 169 to 210. Approximately 440 entries describe books, journal articles and theses which deal with Puerto Rican Spanish. Subject index included.

2.173.   Sarramía, Tomás. "Bibliografía del esperanto en Puerto Rico." **Revista del Instituto de Cultura Puertorriqueña** 94 (In press)

Will be a unique contribution by a respected scholar.

2.174.   Serís, Homero. **Bibliografía de la lingüística española**. Bogotá, Colombia: Imprenta Patriótica del Instituto Caro y Cuervo, 1964. 981 p. (Publicaciones Instituto Caro y Cuervo, 19)

This unannotated bibliography deals with Spanish linguistics in Spanish-speaking countries. The main section on Puerto Rico (pages 784 to 787) has twenty-three references subdivided into the following topics: general studies; lexicography; fauna and flora; toponymy and onomastics.

2.175.   Universidad de Puerto Rico. Colegio de Arecibo. Departmento de Español y Biblioteca. **Bibliografía [sobre el español de Puerto Rico]** Arecibo, P.R.: 1989. 17 p.

This useful unannotated bibliography was prepared as part of the activities of the First National Congress on the Spanish of Puerto Rico. Emphasis is placed on the works of congress participants: Manuel Alvarez Nazario, Robert Hammond, Humberto López, Shana Poplack, Amparo Morales and María Vaquero. Other important relevant works are included. Books and theses, journal articles and some newspaper articles are cited in separate sections. References are not limited to items owned by the library, a fact which increases the value of this contribution.

2.176.   _____ Colegio de Ciencias Sociales.   Social Science Research Center. "Bibliography about Bilingualism." Prepared by Angelina S. de Roca. [Río Piedras, P.R.: 1962] 27 p. (mimeographed)

An annotated work on bilingualism, covering 1950 to 1962. Arranged alphabetically, it includes many references relating to Puerto Ricans on the island as well as on the mainland. A new edition would be of great value in light of new knowledge, controversies and viewpoints.

2.177.   Vaquero, María and Amparo Morales. "El español en Puerto Rico y su enseñanza: recopilación bibliográfica y estado de la cuestión." **Revista de Estudios Hispánicos** (Puerto Rico) 13 (1986): 121-54.

Identifies and analizes three major periods in the teaching of the Spanish language in Puerto Rico: 1900-1942, 1940-1960, and 1960-1977. An alphabetically-arranged bibliography of approximately 274 references follows the discussion. Books, journal articles, government reports and theses fall within the scope of this useful work.

LAW

2.178.   Dávila Lanausse, José Nilo.   **Bibliotheca legum portoricensis, collectanea jurídica; bibliografía legal selecta de Puerto Rico, siglos XIX-XX**. San Juan, P.R.: Colegio de Abogados de Puerto Rico, 1962. 505 p.

The most important and complete bibliography of Puerto Rican law yet published. Its 2,577 entries are arranged alphabetically by author. However, its analytical and jurisprudential indexes facilitate subject access. The work covers the period 1493 to 1958, and includes books, journal articles, pamphlets and unpublished works from Puerto Rico, the United States, Spain and other countries. A new, expanded edition is in preparation and will surely be the most authoritative ever compiled.

2.179.   Delgado Cintrón, Carmelo. "Breve historia de las revistas jurídicas puertorriqueñas." **Revista del Colegio de Abogados de Puerto Rico** 32 (February 1971): 91-101.

Approximately twenty-three legal journals are described in this historical, bibliographic essay. Information given includes: publication data, frequency, type of article and the names of each journal's first directors or organizers. Arranged by the following topics: Spanish antecedents; Puerto Rican legal journals; and **La Revista de Derechos Humanos**.

2.180.   _____.   "Entre libros y papeles: experiencias de un investigador en bibliotecas y archivos españoles y norteamericanos." **Revista del Colegio de Abogados de Puerto Rico** 42 (August 1981): 489-509.

Although the article emphasizes libraries and archives of interest for the study of the history of Puerto Rican law, it also describes specific books and journals.

2.181.   Hernández, Roberto. "Bibliografía anotada Colección Domingo
Toledo Alamo." [Santurce, P.R.: Universidad Interamericana de Puerto Rico,
Facultad de Derecho, Biblioteca, 19??] 36 p. (mimeographed)

> An annotated list of materials found in the Library of the Law Faculty
> at Interamerican University, Santurce Campus. The first part
> describes sources related to law in Puerto Rico: books, journals,
> statutes, codes, decisions and other sources.

2.182.   Noriega, Amarilis. "Bibliografía temática de materiales
audiovisuales disponibles en la Biblioteca." [Santurce, P.R.]: Universidad
Interamericana de Puerto Rico, Facultad de Derecho, Biblioteca, 1987. 49 p.
(mimeographed)

> Although most of the audiovisual materials contained in this topical
> bibliography deal with the United States, there are references to
> Puerto Rican law and related issues. Most items are sound recordings
> of conferences given by distinguished speakers. However some video
> recordings and microforms are included.

2.183.   Siaca Pacheco, Ramón. **Bibliographical Notes on the Law
and Legal Literature of Porto Rico.** New York: American Foreign Law
Association, 1928. 10 p. (Bibliographies of Foreign Law Series, no. 5)

> Contains brief notes on major sources of Puerto Rican law including
> codes and general laws, reports, digests and others.

LIBRARIANSHIP

2.184.   Alamo de Torres, Daisy. "La bibliotecología en Puerto Rico:
fondos   existentes   en   la   Biblioteca   de   la   Escuela   Graduada   de
Bibliotecología."   Río Piedras, P.R.:   Biblioteca, Escuela Graduada de
Bibliotecología, Universidad de Puerto Rico, Recinto de Río Piedras, 1978.
15 p. (mimeographed)

> This bibliography on librarianship in Puerto Rico is divided into the
> following sections: books and pamphlets; an index to **Boletín de la
> Sociedad de Bibliotecarios de Puerto Rico**; miscellaneous;
> audiovisual materials; journal articles.

2.185.   Mi Costa de Ramos, Carmen. "Notes on the Acquisition and
Organization of Government Documents at the Puerto Rican Collection of the
University of Puerto Rico's Campus Library System." In **Latin American
Minorities: Their Images and Realities**, edited by Seminar on the

Acquisition of Latin American Library Materials (39th: 1985: Princeton, N.J.) vol. 2: 422-29. Madison, Wis.: SALALM Secretariat, 1987.

> Although this paper is basically a description of problems and characteristics of the government documents collection at the University of Puerto Rico's General Library, it concludes with a bibliography of Puerto Rican government serial publications and periodicals. Approximately forty publications are cited.

2.186.   Rivera de Bayrón, Vilma. **Bibliografía bibliotecológica: fondos existentes en la Biblioteca de la Escuela Graduada de Bibliotecología**. Río Piedras, P.R.: Biblioteca, Escuela Graduada de Bibliotecología, Depto. de Bibliotecas Graduadas, Biblioteca José M. Lázaro, Universidad de Puerto Rico, 1980. 32 p.

> This specialized bibliography is divided into four parts: books, pamplets, index to **Boletín de la Sociedad de Bibliotecarios de Puerto Rico**, and local newspaper articles. The latter section is arranged chronologically.

2.187.   _____ and Nilda R. Casillas. **Desglose de artículos en periódicos y revistas sobre bibliotecología puertorriqueña, 1942–1979, parte I**. Río Piedras, P.R.: Biblioteca, Escuela Graduada de Bibliotecología, Depto. de Bibliotecas Graduadas, Biblioteca José M. Lázaro, Universidad de Puerto Rico, 1980. 67 p.

> A chronological arrangement characterizes this list which is organized in four sections: 1942-1949; 1950-1959; 1960-1969; and 1 1970-1979. An 1982 supplement of sixteen pages covered 1979 to 1981. The second part, which was to have been a subject index to the first, was never published.

LITERATURE

2.188.   Allen, Richard F. **Teatro hispano-americano: una bibliografía anotada. Spanish American Theatre: An Annotated Bibliography**. Boston: G. K. Hall, 1987. 633 p.

> An annotated bibliography of Latin American plays arranged by country with a preliminary chapter of general anthologies. As well as complete bibliographical descriptions, up to five library location symbols are included for each reference. Asterisks identify one-act plays. The chapter on Puerto Rico has 135 entries, eleven of which

are for anthologies. The author and title indexes should be consulted
in order to locate all entries for a specific work or author.

2.189.   Becco, Horacio Jorge. **Bibliografía general de las artes
del espectáculo en América Latina**. Paris: Unesco, 1977. 118 p.

Includes a section of sixty-two critical studies on Puerto Rican
theater (pages 55 to 58).

2.190.   **Bibliografía general de la literatura latinoamericana**.
Paris: Unesco, 1972. 187 p.

This general bibliography is arranged by region under each of the
following main headings: bibliography of bibliographies; bibliography;
nineteenth century; and contemporary era. Puerto Rico is represented
in all sections except, surprisingly, the contemporary era. Name
index.

2.191.   Bleznick, Donald W. **A Sourcebook for Hispanic Literature
and Language: A Selected, Annotated Guide to Spanish and Spanish
American Bibliography, Literature, Linguistics, Journals and
Other Source Materials**. Philadelphia, Pa.: Temple University Press,
1974. 183 p.

Includes sections on Puerto Rico and Puerto Rican publications. Very
brief annotations describe the scope of each work. Highly selective.

2.192.   Cautiño, Eduardo and Manuel de la Puebla. "Bibliografía."
Mairena 9 (1987): 151-64.

A bibliogrpahy of transcendentalist poetry, divided into two sections.
Part A lists books written by Félix Franco Oppenheimer, Francisco
Lluch Mora, Eugenio Rentas Lucas and Ramón Zapata Acosta. Part B
describes 110 books, journal articles and theses that deal with
transcendentalism and its authors.

2.193.   Coll, Edna. **Indice informativo de la novela hispanoamericana**. Vol. 1. **Las Antillas**. Río Piedras, P.R.: Editorial Universitaria,
Universidad de Puerto Rico, 1974, pp. 29-167.

Identifies the fiction works of Puerto Rican authors from all periods.
Entries are arranged alphabetically by author. Basic biographical
facts or brief biographical sketches are given for each. Many of the
works cited are also accompanied by short summaries and/or critical

comments. In most cases, references are given to other works of
criticism on each author. An important, authoritative and useful book.

2.194.   Engber, Marjorie. **Caribbean Fiction and Poetry**. New York:
Center for Inter-American Relations, 1970. 86 p.

"Designed for students, teachers and scholars", this bibliography includes twenty-four direct references to Puerto Rican fiction and
poetry written from 1900 to 1970 and translated into English.
Additional items can be found in the anthologies section where
contributors are listed for each collection. Four indexes facilitate
checking for specific items or authors.

2.195.   Finch, Mark S.   "A Selective Bibliography on Caribbean
Literature." **Revista/Review Interamericana** 11 (Summer 1981): 283-
300.

Includes an alphabetical section on Puerto Rican literature. The 204
items described are owned by the Inter American University Library,
Metropolitan Campus.

2.196.   Flores, Angel. **Bibliografía de escritores hispano-
americanos. A Bibliography of Spanish-American Writers, 1609-
1974**. New York: Gordian Press, 1975. 318 p.

Puerto Rican authors are included. Under each writer appears a list
of his works, sources of information by and about him, and a selective
list of biographies and criticism in books, journals and theses.

2.197.   Foster, David William.   **Puerto Rican Literature: A
Bibliography of Secondary Sources**. Westport, Conn.: Greenwood Press,
1982. 232 p.

An important, useful work which is organized by topic: bibliographies;
general histories; collected essays; literary criticism, reviews and
journals; literature and other subjects; relations with foreign literatures; women authors; special literary topics; general studies on
colonial literature; general studies on nineteenth century literature;
general studies on twentieth century literature; general studies on
poetry; colonial and nineteenth century poetry; twentieth century
poetry; special topics in poetry; general studies on drama; twentieth
century drama; special topics in drama; general studies on prose
fiction; nineteenth century prose fiction; twentieth century prose
fiction; special topics in prose fiction; general studies on the essay;
critical works on Puerto Rican literature: authors. The latter section

forms the main body of the work. Under each author are listed
bibliographies, monographs and theses, and critical essays (mainly
journal articles). Foster excludes "journalistic" articles and has
selected academic and cultural criticisms that he believes best serve
the interests of academic literary scholars.

2.198.   Freudenthal, Juan R. and Patricia M. Freudenthal. **Index to
Anthologies of Latin American Literature in English Translation.**
Boston: G. K. Hall, 1977. 199 p.

The geographic index provides access to more than seventy Puerto
Rican authors whose works have been included in English-language
anthologies of Latin American literature. Under each author references are made to each anthology where a work appears.

2.199.   González Monclova, Nilda. **Bibliografía del teatro puertorriqueño: siglos XIX y XX.** Río Piedras, P.R.: Editorial Universitaria,
Universidad de Puerto Rico, 1979. 223 p.

One of the most complete bibliographies on the Puerto Rican theatre
yet published. The introduction offers an historical perspective of
Puerto Rico's rich dramatical tradition, as well as explaining the
book's organization and scope. The main section of the bibliography
is arranged alphabetically by dramatist. Under each name appear
references to works written by the author. Following each title,
further references are given for criticisms and commentaries of each.
The next section of the book lists collective works. A series of
useful appendixes completes the book: zarzuelas and operas; works
for which complete references are not available, according to the
Emilio J. Pasarell collection; works from the bohemian "farándula";
the Institute of Puerto Rican Culture's theatre festivals (1958-1976);
unpublished manuscripts in the Office of Theatre Development at the
Institute of Puerto Rican Culture; award-winning works in the
Ateneo's theatre competitions (1913-1976); theatre companies
(1931-1976); pseudonyms. Author and title indexes are provided.

2.200.   _____ "Bibliografía mínima de teatro puertorriqueño."
Revista del Instituto de Cultura Puertorriqueña 20 (July-December
1977): 128-32.

This selective, unannotated bibliography has four sections: works by
dramatist arranged by century (19th and 20th); historical studies;
books of essays on Puerto Rican drama; and bibliographies. This
article is illustrated.

2.201.   Hebblethwaite, Frank P. **A Bibliographical Guide to Spanish American Theater.** Washington, D.C.: Pan American Union, 1969. 84 p. (Basic Bibliographies, VI)

> Covers material on the history and criticism of the Spanish American theater. It includes references to Puerto Rican theatre under "Books: Sources by country" and under "Articles: Sources by country."

2.202.   Hernández Vargas, Nélida. "Don Federico de Onís y los puertorriqueños: bibliografía y noticias." **Revista de Estudios Hispánicos** (Puerto Rico) 12 (1985): 73-80.

> This unannotated list emphasizes Federico de Onís' interpretation of Puerto Rican literature in the American context. The first section of the bibliography describes works by Onís on Puerto Rican authors or themes (eighteen items). The following section of seventy-five citations lists critical studies and tributes to Federico de Onís. A third part provides a chronological list of news items and activities that reflect the author's relations with the University of Puerto Rico and the Puerto Rican people.

2.203.   Hill, Marnesba D. and Harold B. Schleifer. **Puerto Rican Authors: A Biobibliographical Handbook. Autores puertorriqueños: una guía biobibliográfica.** With an introduction by María Teresa Babín. Translations of entries into Spanish by Daniel Maratos. Metuchen, N.J.: Scarecrow Press, 1974. 267 p.

> Not intended to be an exhaustive scholarly work, this is a useful bi-lingual guide to Puerto Rican history and literature as written by Puerto Ricans. It is arranged alphabetically by author, for each of which biographical information is given first. An alphabetical list of the author's works is followed by brief annotations or comments for some of them. Three indexes are appended: topic (that is, genre and/or occupation), historical periods and title.

2.204.   Hulet, Claude L. **Latin American Poetry in English Translation: A Bibliography.** Washington, D.C.: Pan American Union, 1965. 192 p. (Basic Bibliographies, II)

> Pages 155 to 158 contain references to sixty-three works of Puerto Rican poetry translated into English. Journal titles are abbreviated and can be found in a list provided at the end of the book.

2.205.   Hulet, Claude L. . **Latin American Prose in English Translation: A Bibliography**. Washington, D.C.: Pan American Union, 1964. 191 p.

References to works of Puerto Rican prose authors translated into English appear under the following headings: essay, history, literary criticism, novel and short story. Not annotated.

2.206.   Kirschner, Madeline. "Puerto Rican Bibliography." **RQ** 9 (Fall 1969): 9-19.

This briefly annotated bibliography cites 240 novels, plays, biographies, essays, histories, works of poetry, literary criticisms and books of folklore which can be found in the Brooklyn Public Library System. Asterisks identify 100 titles considered to be basic items for a Spanish-language collection in a medium-sized library. A list of publishers and distributors is appended.

2.207.   Labandeira Fernández, Amancio. "Cubanos y puertorriqueños que deben figurar en un 'Catálogo de novelas y novelistas españoles del siglo XIX': identificaciones y precisiones." **Anales de Literatura Hispanoamericana** 11 (1982): 51-73.

Although the emphasis is on Cubans, some Puerto Ricans are dealt with. The work is meant to supplement Juan Ignacio Ferrera's **Catálogo de novelas y novelistas españoles del siglo XIX**. For each author, brief biographical data accompanies the list of works.

2.208.   Lyday, Leon F. and George W. Woodyard. **A Bibliography of Latin American Theater Criticism, 1940-1974**. Austin, Tex.: Institute of Latin American Studies, University of Texas at Austin, 1976. 243 p.

Arranged alphabetically by critical author, this bibliography includes about seventy-six references to Puerto Rican drama and dramatists. The topical index may be consulted for references to criticisms of specific dramatists or one may look for the appropriate geographical reference which is found to the right of each citation. Partially annotated.

2.209.   Mohr, Eugene. "Fifty Years of Puerto Rican Literature in English: 1923-1973; An Annotated Bibliography." **Revista/Review Interamericana** 3 (Fall 1973): 290-98.

This is a briefly annotated record of literature in English written by continentals living in Puerto Rico and by Puerto Ricans living on the mainland. Material published only in periodicals is not included. The bibliography is organized chronologically by date of publication under the following categories: poems, novels, autobiographies, para-literary additions, translations and periodicals.

2.210.   Montalvo Montalvo, Marilyn. **Poesía puertorriqueña en las colecciones del Colegio Universitario del Turabo: bibliografía**. Gurabo, P.R.: Centro de Recursos de Aprendizaje, 1977. 91 p.

Divided into two main divisions, this list cites works of poetry in the Turabo University College Library. The general works division lists general criticisms and anthologies. In the second part, entries are arranged alphabetically by poet. Each work is followed by the corresponding criticisms that can be found in the library.

2.211.   Pérez Morales, Carlos. **El genero "novela" en la Colección Puertorriqueña del Colegio Universitario de Humacao: guía bibliográfica**.   Humacao, P.R.:   Colegio Universitario de Humacao, Biblioteca, 1984. 20 p. (Mundo bibliográfico, 2nd year, no. 1)

Following a brief history of the Puerto Rican novel, Pérez divides his bibliography in three areas: novels, listed alphabetically by author; critical studies; and general sources on Puerto Rican literature. A useful index to criticisms of specific authors completes the work.

2.212.   Perrier, Joseph Luis. **Bibliografía dramática cubana, incluye a Puerto Rico y Santo Domingo**. New York: Phos Press, 1926. 115 p.

The appendix found on pages 109 to 115 provides bibliographical data on fifty-seven Puerto Rican dramas. Much of the information was supplied by Cayetano Coll y Toste.

2.213.   Piñeiro de Rivera, Flor and Isabel Freire de Matos. **Literatura infantil caribeña: Puerto Rico, República Dominicana y Cuba**. Hato Rey, P.R.: Boriken, 1983. 123 p.

This title is included for its bibliography of Puerto Rican childrens' literature which is to be found on pages 26 to 30. Unannotated but fairly unique.

2.214.   "Poesía 1979 en Puerto Rico." **Mairena** 1 (Christmas 1979): 74-88.

Describes books of poetry published during the year. A poem from each one is reproduced.

2.215.   "Poesía puertorriqueña (libros publicados en 1982)." **Mairena** 5 (Spring 1983): 85-111.

A representative poem complements each citation for poetry books published in 1983 in Puerto Rico.

2.216.   Puebla, Manuel de la. "Notas en torno a la bibliografía sobre Palés." **Mairena** 1 (Spring 1979): 77-91.

An evaluative bibliographic essay on criticism of the prominent Puerto Rican poet, Luis Palés Matos. The author describes works written by critics from 1917 to the late 1970s, selecting those of greatest importance or value. Puebla concludes that in spite of the great body of literature in existence, Palés' works are still open for new investigations and perspectives.

2.217.   Quiles de la Luz, Lillian. "Indice bibliográfico del cuento en la literatura puertorriqueña (1843-1963)." In her **El cuento en la literatura puertorriqueña**, 14-293. Río Piedras, P.R.: Editorial U.P.R., Universidad de Puerto Rico, 1968.

Serves as a bibliography of the Puerto Rican short story in books, magazines and anthologies. A title index assures the usefulness of this unique source.

2.218.   Rela, Walter. **Guía bibliográfica de la literatura hispano americana, desde el siglo XIX hasta 1970.** Buenos Aires, Argentina: Casa Pardo, 1971. 613 p.

The main body of the work consists of the following divisions: general bibliographies; national bibliographies (including twelve on Puerto Rico); individual bibliographies (including Hostos); general literary histories; national literary histories (eight items on Puerto Rico); essay, history and criticism (including twenty-four references to Puerto Rico); essay, history and criticism on individuals (among them Hostos, Rosendo Matienzo Cintrón, and Luis Palés Matos); general anthologies; national anthologies (including twenty-eight Puerto Rican works); anthologies of individual authors (including islanders); collective biographies; individual biographies; dictionaries; and miscellaneous works. A name index is appended.

2.219.   Rivera de Alvarez, Josefina. **Diccionario de literatura puertorriqueña**. 2d rev. ed. 2 vols in 3   San Juan, P.R.:   Instituto de Cultura Puertorriqueña, 1970-1974.

   The second volume of this work is a bio-bibliographical dictionary of Puerto Rican authors from all fields and periods. After the bio-grahical information and critical comments on each author, biblio-graphical references to the authors works are listed as are citations to criticisms of the author and his work. This is a basic source.

2.220.   Robinson, Barbara J. **Doctoral Dissertations in Hispanic American Literature: A Bibliography of Dissertations Completed in the United States (1964-1974)**. Austin, Tex.: SALALM Secretariat, 1979.   45 p.   (Seminar on the Acquisition of Latin American Library Materials. Bibliography, no. 5)

   "This bibliography is limited to those doctoral dissertations listed in available published sources." It is organized alphabetically by author with indexes by institution, year and country. Twelve entries deal with Puerto Rico.

2.221.   Rosa Nieves, Cesáreo. **Indice bibliográfico para la poesía en Puerto Rico (1682-1942)**. Mexico: 1943. 67 p.

   An important work which describes literary almanacs, anthologies, poetry anthologies, collections of prose and poetry and books of poetry written by individuals during the period indicated.

2.222.   Seidel, Robert N. **Abroad with Translators: Annotated Bibliographies with Introductory Essays on Latin American Literature and Society for the English Language Reader and Student**. With a bibliographical essay on Puerto Rico by Robert Mac Cameron. New York: Empire State College, State University of New York, 1977. 42 p. (ED 147 357)

   Mac Cameron's essay identifies ten major Puerto Rican authors whose works have been translated into English. He gives publication data for each of these works. Nine other references are given for non-fiction works about Puerto Rico.

2.223.   Simmons, Merle E. **A Bibliography of the Romance and Related Forms in Spanish America**. Bloomington, Ind.:   Indiana University Press, 1963. 396 p.

   A small section covers popular poetry and song in Puerto Rico.

Twenty briefly annotated entries are arrranged chronologically from 1920, the year in which María Cadilla's pioneering work was published, to 1939.

2.224.   Sotomayor, Aurea María. "Bibliografía de la promoción del '70." **Reintegro** 3 (April 1983): 20, 24 (extra).

Unannotated, this list cites works by and about thirteen poets of the 1970s: Vanessa Droz, Obed Edom, Servando Echeandía, Gina de Lucca, Jan Martínez, Joserramón Melendes, Nemir Matos Cintrón, Roberto Net Carlo, Luz Ivonne Ochart, Lilliana Ramos Collado, Arnaldo Sepúlveda, Aurea María Sotomayor and Angel Luis Torres.

2.225.   Universidad de Puerto Rico. Biblioteca y Hermeroteca Puertorriqueña. "Puerto Rican Literature: Translations into English. Literatura puertorriqueña: traducciones al inglés." Río Piedras, P.R.: 1974. 38 p. (mimeographed)

Cites literary works which have been translated into English. The arrangement is alphabetical under the following genres: short story; short stories for young people; essay; novel, poetry; and drama. A list of abbreviations is included for anthologies, newspapers and journals cited. Indexes are by author, Spanish titles and English titles.

2.226.   Vigo-Cepeda, Luisa. "Recursos bibliográficos para la investigación de la literatura del Caribe hispanoparlante: literatura puertorriqueña." In **Los recursos bibliotecarios para la investigación en el Caribe: documentos oficiales,** edited by Conferencia Anual de ACURIL (3rd.: 1971: Caracas, Venezuela), 305-319. San Juan, P.R.: Asociación de Bibliotecas Universitarias y de Investigación del Caribe, 1978.

Constitutes a bibliographic essay which touches upon the following topics: introduction; historical background; reference sources; special collections; institute dedicated to promoting literature; list of libraries specializing in Puerto Rican literature; and general references and recommendations.

2.227.   Ward, James. "A Tentative Inventory of Young Puerto Rican Writers." **Hispania** 54 (December 1971): 924-30.

A bibliographic essay which discusses young Puerto Rican authors under thirty years of age. The information given for each one includes biographical data and a description of their literary works.

2.228.   Woodbridge, Hensley. **Spanish and Spanish American Literature: An Annotated Guide to Selected Bibliographies**. New York: The Modern Language Association of America, 1983. 74 p.

The small section on Puerto Rico includes brief descriptions of ten well-known bibliographies in no apparent order. The general section on Latin American literature might also be consulted.

2.229.   Woodyard, George W. and Leon F. Lyday.   "Studies on Latin American Theatre." **Theatre Documentation** 2 (1967-1970): 49-84.

Cites works published between 1960 and 1969, a decade which "witnessed an unprecedented flourishing in the theatre arts of Latin America." Includes critical studies which appeared in journals, books, doctoral dissertations and reviews. Items are organized alphabetically but the nationality of the author studied is indicated in the margin, thus making it easy to locate the thirty-seven references to Puerto Rican theater. Moreover, an index to dramatists is included.

MEDICINE AND HEALTH

2.230.   **Bibliografía sobre enfermería**. Mayagüez, P.R.: Biblioteca General, Recinto Universitario de Mayagüez, Universidad de Puerto Rico, 1981. 158 p. (Cuadernos bibliográficos en el RUM, 1)

Organized by topics, this list includes sections on material published in Puerto Rican journals and newspapers. It covers diseases and general aspects of health and medicine, as well as nursing. Many items deal specifically with Puerto Rican themes. A supplement of 106 pages was published in 1982 and follows the same format as the original volume.

2.231.   Ferguson, F. F.   **Bibliografía seleccionada sobre la bilharzia antillana, o esquistosomiasis mansoni**. San Juan, P.R.: Talleres de Artes Gráficas del Departamento de Instrucción Pública, 1958. 66 p.

Although somewhat dated, this publication contains numerous references to the problem and its treatment on the island. Bilharzia was one of the major health problems on the island for many decades.

2.232.   United States. Department of Health, Education and Welfare. Regional Medical Programs Service. **Selected Bibliography of Regional**

Medical Programs. Washington, D.C.: Health Services and Mental Health
Administration, 1968-

> Includes citations and brief descriptions of the publications of the
> Puerto Rico Regional Medical Programs. At least three editions have
> been issued.

2.233.   University of Puerto Rico.   School of Medicine.   "List of
Publications 1950-1965." Río Piedras, P.R.: 1965? 144 p. (mimeographed)

> Lists all types of publications by the faculty members of the Medical
> Sciences Campus. Many of them deal with some aspect of medicine or
> health in Puerto Rico. However, the lack of a subject index makes it
> difficult to identify them. The only index is to co-authors. An up-
> dated edition of this publication would be more helpful.

2.234.   _____ _____ Library. "Bilharzia (Schistosomiasis
mansoni) in Puerto Rico: A Bibliography, 1904-1962." San Juan, P.R.: 1963.
18 p. (mimeogrphed)

> Unannotated list of 271 journal articles on the subject. In 1965, a
> supplemental list of thirty-six additional references was issued.
> Compiled by Lillian Casas de López, the bibliography incorporates an
> earlier one prepared in 1955. Entries cite English, French and Spanish
> materials on a serious health problem which affected the island's
> inhabitants for many decades. It may be used to supplement a simi-
> lar work compiled by Ferguson (2.231).

2.235.   _____. _____. _____ "Catalogue of Publications
in the Ashford Collection at the School of Medicine Library." San Juan, P.R.:
School of Medicine, Library, 1961. 16 p. (mimeographed)

> Although many books included are general medical references, the
> bibliography does have a section of works written by Dr. Bailey
> Ashford, many of which deal with Puerto Rican matters. Ashford, a
> distinguished doctor and scientist, worked in Puerto Rico for many
> years and made pioneering efforts in many scientific areas.

MUNICIPALITIES

2.236.   Anderson, Víctor D.   **Bibliografía municipal geográfica
puertorriqueña**. Río Piedras, P.R.: Editorial Universitaria, 1980. 147 p.

> This important work covers books, journal and newspaper articles,

government documents and theses. The first part cites general references on Puerto Rico's municipalities or references dealing with several towns. The second part is arranged alphabetically by towns. Abbreviations indicate one or more libraries having a copy of each item. This is an important starting point for the study of any Puerto Rican town.

2.237.   Carmona Romay, Adriano G. "Bibliografía general sobre el tema de los municipios puertorriqueños (desde sus orígenes a nuestros días)." Río Piedras, P.R.: 1960. 41 p. (mimeographed)

References in this general bibliography on Puerto Rican municipalities appear under the following topics: Puerto Rico's constitutions; legislation, municipal government and law; commentary on mainland laws; accounting; miscellaneous; Eugneio María de Hostos' thoughts on municipalities; general works on public administration; bibliography in progress; theses and essays of the School of Public Administration; University of Puerto Rico programs related to municipal government; personnel; finances; taxes; urban development and planning; history of the capital; and others.

2.238.   **Catálogo de documentos históricos de Bayamón**. Edited by Ignacio Olazagasti. 8 vols. in 14 Bayamón, P.R.: Instituto de Histroia y Cultura de Bayamón, 1979-1982.

Almost all entries in this extensive bibliography describe primary sources kept at the General Archives of Puerto Rico. Contents: v.1, Public works; v.2, Spanish governors; v.3, Historic fund of the Fortaleza; v.4, part 1, Journals and newspapers of the Robert L. Junghanns Collection in the General Archives of Puerto Rico; v.4, part 2, Folklore materials in the Robert L. Junghanns Collection; v.4, part 3, Documents in the Robert L. Junghanns Collection; v.4, part 4, Folkloric stories in the Robert L. Junghanns Collection; v.4, part 5, New folklore materials in the Robert L. Junghanns Collection; v.4, part 6, Record collection of the Robert L. Junghanns Collection; v.4, part 7, Books in the Robert L. Junghanns Collection; v.5, Provincial Delegation; v.6, Historical documents in the National Archives, Madrid, Spain; v.7, Municipal fund under Spanish sovereignty; v.8, Basic bibliography of the city of Bayamón. The latter part in itself is a bibliography of Bayamón and covers secondary sources.

2.239.   Cuebas Irizarry, Ana E. **En busca de una bibliografía para Mayagüez**. Mayagüez, P.R.: Centro Cultural Eugenio María de Hostos, 1984. 13 p.

Intended as a basic, preliminary bibliography of the city of Mayagüez, it is organized in four sections: information in general and specialized encyclopedias, monographs, journal and newspaper articles, and others. Annotated.

2.240.   Fowlie-Flores, Fay. **Ponce, Perla del Sur: una bibliografía anotada.** Ponce, P.R.: Centro de Estudios Puertorriqueños, Universidad de Puerto Rico en Ponce, 1988. 217 p.

This alphabetically-arranged bibliography describes books, articles, government documents, pamphlets and other materials which deal with some aspect of the city of Ponce. The purpose of the work is to reflect the city's social, cultural, political and economic heritage and to serve as a starting point for those interested in investigating and understanding Ponce's past and present.. The length of the annotations reflects the importance or complexity of each entry. Locations are indicated for each item, except articles from daily newspapers. Author, title and subject indexes are included, and refer to the item number.

2.241.   "Hemerografía sobre historia municipal y regional de Puerto Rico." **Boletín de Historia Puertorriqueña** 1 (March 1949): 107-108.

A short list of references to articles published in newspapers or journals on the founding of certain towns in Puerto Rico. All articles cited were written by G. E. Morales Muñoz. Several entries are dupli-cated by entry under the town's original name and its present name.

2.242.   Hernández Paralitici, Pedro H.   **Bibliografía utuadeña: 1880-1980.** Utuado, P.R.: Editorial Ubec, 1980. 50 p.

This unannotated list cites works written about the town of Utuado or by its citizens. Works of literature are included. Arranged alpha-betically by author but lacks an undex.

2.243.   Pasarell, Emilio S.   "Notas bibliográficas acerca de los periódicos de Ponce." **El Mundo**, 18 August 1935, pp. 2, 4, 12.

A chronological, annotated list of 230 newspapers founded in the city of Ponce from 1848 to 1934. The author claims to rectify some errors in other works by Coll y Toste, Neumann Gandía, Miller and others. Asterisks identify especially influential, important and/or path-breaking newspapers.

POLITICS, GOVERNMENT AND PUBLIC ADMINISTRATION

2.244.   Anderson, Víctor D. "Elecciones y política en Puerto Rico." Río Piedras, P.R.: Biblioteca, Escuela Graduada de Administración Pública, Departamento de Bibliotecas Graduadas, Biblioteca José M. Lázaro, Universidad de Puerto Rico, 1978. 33 p. (mimeographed)

> Each of the two parts of this work is organized alphabetically by author. The first section deals with elections in Puerto Rico while the second part covers politics in general. A location is given for each item cited. A revised edition would be most helpful.

2.245.   Chilcote, Ronald H. **Revolution and Structural Change in Latin America: A Bibliography on Ideology, Development, and the Radical Left (1930-1965)**. 2 vols. Stanford, Calif.: The Hoover Institution on War, Revolution and Peace, Standford University, 1970.

> "The emphasis of this bibliography is upon traditional and emerging leftist political forces of Latin American society and their approaches to a theory of structural change." Puerto Rican leftist and pro-independence movements are treated in the section on the Caribbean (pages 451 to 463). Approximately thirty-one references are included to books, articles, theses and newspapers. Author, subject and periodical indexes increase the usefulness of this book.

2.246.   Cruz Colón, José Antonio. "Bibliografía sobre literatura de administración pública relacionada con Puerto Rico (1898-1966)." Master's thesis, University of Puerto Rico, 1961.

> References to public administration in Puerto Rico are organized by format under twenty-three topics. No indexes are included.

2.247.   Dahlin, Therrin C., Gary P. Gillum and Mark L. Grover. **The Catholic Left in Latin America: A Comprehensive Bibliography**. Boston: G. K. Hall, 1981. 410 p.

> Within the geographic arrangement of this bibliography on the Catholic Left movement in Latin America, references to Puerto Rico can be found in the chapter on the Caribbean. This section is subdivided by topics (pages 217 to 222).

2.248.   **Foreign Affairs Bibliography: A Selected and Annotated List of Books on International Relations, 1919/32-1952/62**. 4 vols. New York: Harper, 1933-1964.

Publisher varies. Short annotations describe English-language
sources on Puerto Rico in each edition. Cross references indicate
other related topics. Based mainly on information taken from the
journal **Foreign Affairs**. Henry L. Roberts edited several editions.

2.249.   Geigel Polanco, Vicente. "Bibliografía mínima-status político
de Puerto Rico." **Revista de Derecho, Legislación y Jurisprudencia
del Colegio de Abogados de Puerto Rico** 8 (July-September 1945):
241-43.

   A short, selective, unannotated bibliography on the political status of
   the island by an authoritative compiler. For a more recent work see
   Altagracia Miranda's compilation (2.254).

2.250.   Goldsmith, William W., Pierre Clavel and Deborah Roth.   "A
Bibliography on Public Planning in Puerto Rico."   **Latin American
Research Review** 9 (Summer 1974): 143-69.

   A brief history of planning in Puerto Rico, a definition of planning and
   an explanation of the bibliography provide an introduction to this
   work. The main sections are: general works; economic planning and
   development; social planning and development; urban and rural development; reference works. Location symbols are provided for unpublished material, reports and pamphlets. All sections except the
   first and last are subdivided by books and theses, articles and
   pamphlets, reports and unpublished items. This bibliography was also
   reprinted as occasional paper number five of the Cornell University
   Center for Urban Development Research.

2.251.   Kidder, Frederick E. "Puerto Rican Politics in Graduate Studies."
Ciencias Políticas en Puerto Rico 1 (May 1962): 7-11.

   Unannotated and selective, this list describes masters and doctoral
   theses written at American universities on Puerto Rico's government
   and politics. Arranged chronologically.

2.252.   _____   "Government and Politics of Puerto Rico: A Five
Foot Shelf." **Ciencias Políticas en Puerto Rico** 1 (November 1962):
14-15; 1 (February 1963): 19-21.

   Kidder provides a list of titles which he considers to be fundamental
   for the study of government and politics in Puerto Rico.

2.253.   Lauerhass, Ludwig, Jr. **Communism in Latin America: A
Bibliography; the Post-War Years (1945-1960)**. Los Angleles, Calif.:

Center of Latin American Studies, University of California, 1962. 78 p.

Includes fourteen references to books, government publications and journal articles on communism in Puerto Rico during the period mentioned.

2.254.   Miranda, Altagracia. **El status político de Puerto Rico, 1952-1983: bibliografía de libros y artículos de revistas que se encuentran en la Biblioteca de Derecho de la Universidad de Puerto Rico**. San Juan, P.R.: Biblioteca de Derecho, Universidad de Puerto Rico, 1984. 15 p.

A useful bibliography of materials on Puerto Rico's political status, an issue of continuing importance. The first section (books) is arranged alphabetically while the second part (journal articles) is organized chronologically.

2.255.   Ocampo, Tarsicio. **Puerto Rico Partido Acción Cristiana, 1960-62: documentos y reacciones de prensa**. Cuernavaca, Mexico: Centro Intercultural de Documentación, 1967.   1 vol. (various pagings) (CIDOC Dossier, 11)

Chronologically arranged bibliography of the controversy surrounding the creation of a new political party, the Partido de Acción Cristiana. The first period, 1941 to 1953, covers the controversy on birth control and religious education on the island. The second period includes the press coverage from March to September of 1960 when the party was created; part three deals with October and November of 1960 with emphasis on political manifestos and pastoral letters. The next section deals with the post-electoral period, especially the impact of the new party on the older ones, from November of 1960 to November of 1962. A final section of the bibliography cites references taken from another work ("La iglesia y el estado en Puerto Rico," a thesis by Benjamín Santana Jiménez).

2.256.   Orduña Rebollo, Enrique. **Bibliografía iberoamericana de administración local**. Caracas, Venezuela: Asociación Venezolana de Cooperación Intermunicipal, Instituto de Estudios de Administración Local, 1983. 813 p.

Arranged topically, this bibliography has author, subject and geographic indexes. The latter facilitates the location of the many references included for Puerto Rico. Books and journal articles are cited.

2.257.   Torres Irizarry, Martha E. **Bibliografía de proyectos de planificación: 1968-1978.** Río Piedras, P.R.: Universidad de Puerto Rico, Recinto de Río Piedras, Biblioteca General, Departamento de Bibliotecas Graduadas, Biblioteca de la Escuela Graduada de Planificación, 1979. 66 p.

A bibliography of planning projects presented by graduate students of the Graduate School of Planning as a prerequisite for graduation. Divided by author, title and subject. The projects constitute plans to solve a particular problem, the majority of which refer to Puerto Rican situations.

2.258.   Torres Tapia, Manuel. **El ombudsman: ensayo bibliográfico.** San Juan, P.R.: Sociedad de Bibliotecarios de Puerto Rico, 1977. 45 p. (Cuadernos bibliográficos, 1)

This bibliography deals with the office of ombudsman in general and with that office in Puerto Rico.

2.259.   _____. **Ombudsmanship in Puerto Rico: A Bibliography.** Monticello, Ill.: Vance Bibliographies, 1984. 33 p. (Public Administration Series: Bibliography P-1487)

Citations appear in chronological order under the following: bills and resolutions; legislative procedures and debates; public hearings; speeches; reports and memoranda; statutes; opinions of the Secretary of Justice; monographs, dissertations, etc.; journal and press articles; bibliographies. The contents, a brief introduction and all headings appear in both English and Spanish. Not annotated.

2.260.   _____. **Ombudsmanship in Puerto Rico: A Bibliography, Part II.** Monticello, Ill.: Vance Bibliographies, 1988. 11 p. (Public Administration Series: Bibliography P2363)

Updates the 1984 edition with seventy-five new references. Unannotated entries are arranged chronologically under the following headings: bills; legislative procedures; reports and memoranda; statutes; journals and press articles; bibliographies; reviews and annotations (of the first edition); and audiovisual materials. Bilingual contents and introduction.

2.261.   United States-Puerto Rico Commission on the Status of Puerto Rico. **Status of Puerto Rico: Report of the United States-Puerto Rico Commission on the Status of Puerto Rico.** Washington, D.C.: Government Printing Office, 1966. 273 p.

Among the appendexes of the Commissions' report of conclusions and recommendations, is an extensive, selective bibliography (pages 235 to 273). English and Spanish studies included are divided into five sections: legal-constitutional; political; economic; social-cultural-historical; and government publications. A very useful source. A Spanish edition (**Status de Puerto Rico; Informe de la Comisión de los Estados Unidos y Puerto Rico sobre el status de Puerto Rico**) was published by the Office of the Commonwealth of Puerto Rico in Washington. In that translation the bibliography appears on pages 243 to 282.

2.262.   United States-Puerto Rico Commission on the Status of Puerto Rico.   **Status of Puerto Rico: Selected Background Studies Prepared for the United States-Puerto Rico Commission on the Status of Puerto Rico**. Washington, D.C.: U.S. Government Printing Office, 1966. 973 p.

Includes ten background studies prepared to foment a "better under-standing of the factors affecting the United States-Puerto Rico re-lationship." With one exception, all studies include bibliographical references and/or bibliographies. Among the most significant bibli-ographies are those appended to the following studies: "Historical Survey of the Puerto Rico Status Question, 1898-1965," by Robert J. Hunter (pages 132-42); "Significant Factors in the Development of Education in Puerto Rico," by Ismael Rodríguez Bou (pages 279-83); "Unionism and Politics in Puerto Rico," by William Knowles (pages 336-38); "Puerto Rico: An Essay in the Definition of a National Culture," by Sidney W. Mintz (pages 431-34); and "Toward a Balance Sheet of Puerto Rican Migration," by Clarence Senior and Donald O. Watkins. The latter is an annotated, selective bibliography divided in two parts: the first consists of articles, essays, reports, speeches and surveys; the second covers books.

2.263.   Universidad de Puerto Rico. Escuela de Administración Pública. **Tesis presentadas para el grado de maestro en administración pública**. Río Piedras, P.R.: 1971. 26 p.

This list of theses in the area of public administration is arranged by subtopic, then alphabetically by author. The entries cite author, title and year of publication.

SCIENCE AND TECHNOLOGY

2.264.   Almodóvar, Luis R.   "Bibliografía sobre botánica marina en Puerto Rico." **Science-Ciencia: Boletín Científico del Sur** 6 (Spring 1979): 126-29.

> Attempts to be as comprehensive as possible to 1978. This alphabetical list has over 100 references pertaining to the marine botany of Puerto Rico.

2.265.   Ayala, Alejandro and Carmen T. Ramírez.   "Host Range, Distribution, and Bibliography of the Reniform Nematode, Rotylenchulus reniformis, with Special Reference to Puerto Rico." **The Journal of Agriculture of the University of Puerto Rico** 48 (April 1964): 140-61.

> As well as describing the geographic distribution of the parasite in the tropics and warm parts of the temperate zone, this article reviews the literature on the parasite in Puerto Rico and includes a bibliography of eighty-nine citations.

2.266.   Ayala Gallisá, Z. de.   **Resumen bibliográfico de los trabajos de investigación de la Planta Piloto de Ron de la Estación Experimental Agrícola de la Universidad de Puerto Rico, 1945-1983.** Río Piedras, P.R.: Estación Experimental Agrícola, Colegio de Ciencias Agrícolas, Recinto de Mayagüez, Universidad de Puerto Rico, 1983. 58 p. (PPR 24-84)

> Spanish-language summaries of research reports constitute the annotations of this topically-arranged bibliography which covers all aspects of rum distilling: general considerations, raw materials, microbiological studies, fermentation, distillation, aging, methodology, final product and wastes.

2.267.   Britton, N. L.   and Percy Wilson.   "Published Botanical Bibliography, Porto Rico and the Virgin Islands: Spermatophyta and Pteridophyta." In **Scientific Survey of Porto Rico and the Virgin Islands,** vol. 6, part 4, 576-82. New York: New York Academy of Sciences, 1930.

> Brief descriptions accompany the references in this work which excludes general works and monographs. Most of the 100 entries deal with these species in Puerto Rico.

2.268.   Brown, Sandra et al. **Research History and Opportunities in the Luquillo Experimental Forest.** New Orleans,La.: U.S. Department of Agriculture, Forest Service, Southern Forest Experiment Station, 1983. 123 p. (General Technical Report SO-44)

This bibliographical study "is aimed at summarizing major findings of the research activity in Luquillo Experimental Forest." It is also hoped that further research opportunities will thereby become apparent. After a general introduction to the rainforest and to current and proposed uses of it, the authors give detailed descriptions of studies which have been done on the area in terms of land use, climate, surface hydrology, water quality of rivers, geology, soils, vegetation, fauna and disturbances. The literature cited section (pages 120 to 128) give complete bibliographic information for all studies mentioned.

2.269.   Caribbean Commission. Caribbean Research Council. Committee on Agriculture, Nutrition, Fisheries and Forestry.   **Forest Research within the Caribbean Area.** Washington, D.C.: 1947. 128 p.

Studies the present status and future needs of forestry research in the Caribbean countries. The bibliography includes fourteen references to the situation in Puerto Rico. Largely of historical interest.

2.270.   Colom Covas, Guillermo. **Contribuciones a la literatura sobre el cultivo, manejo e industrialización del plátano.**   Río Piedras, P.R.: Estación Experimental Agrícola, Recinto Universitario de Mayagüez, Biblioteca, 1971. 6 p. (Lista bibliográfica, 3)

Cites sixty-six references to plantain cultivation and production on the island. Most enties are for journal aritcles.

2.271.   Díaz Piferrer, Manuel. "Adiciones a la flora marina de Puerto Rico." **Caribbean Journal of Science** 3 (December 1963): 215-35.

The history of the literature of marine flora in Puerto Rico is traced in this bibliographic essay. Also included is a taxonomic list of species with corresponding references. Complete bibliographic information is given in the literature cited section.

2.272.   Fink, L. K. Jr. **Regional Bibliography of Caribbean Geology.** Miami, Fla.: Institute of Marine Science, The Marine Laboratory, University of Miami, 1964. 65 p. (Technical Report, 64-3)

This selective bibliography of articles and maps has a section on the geology of Puerto Rico and the Virgin Islands (pages 54 to 64).

2.273.   Freytes, Manuel J. and Luis R. Almodóvar. "Botánica marina en Puerto Rico: bibliografía." **Science-Ciencia: Boletín Científico del Sur** 13 (Winter 1986): 13-20.

Cites seventy-six references dealing with the marine botany of Puerto Rico up to 1985. Of these, forty-eight are theses and dissertations. Unannotated.

2.274.   Gutiérrez Sánchez, Jaime. **Bibliografía comentada sobre la pesca y las localidades pesqueras en Puerto Rico.** Mayagüez, P.R.: Programa Sea Grant, Universidad de Puerto Rico, Recinto Universitario de Mayagüez, 1985. 29 p.

Covers ninety-four publications related to fishermen, production and fishing sites in Puerto Rico. Excludes material dealing with recreational and inland water fishing. Annotations for this alphbetically-arranged bibliography are given in the language of the publication described. No topic index (Also published in **Atenea** (Mayagüez) 3rd series 4 (June-December 1984): 167-97.)

2.275.   Hayes, Joan P. "Lista de tesis catalogadas en la Biblioteca de la Estación Experimental Agrícola." Río Piedras, P.R.: Universidad de Puerto Rico,   Estación   Experimental   Agrícola,   Biblioteca,   1970.   4   p. (mimeographed)

Includes fifty-seven masters and doctoral theses owned by the Library. Many deal with situations in Puerto Rico.

2.276.   Hernández, Lucy and Ricardo Riccardi. **Bibliografía sobre los manglares en Puerto Rico.** San Juan, P.R.: Departamento de Recursos Naturales, Oficina de Planificación de Recursos Forestales, 1978. 31 p.

An unannotated bibliography of 357 references to Puerto Rico's mangroves. Covers biological and ecological aspects. No expanatory introduction nor indexes are included.

2.277.   Hooker, Marjorie. **Bibliography and Index of the Geology of Puerto Rico and Vicinity, 1866-1968.** San Juan, P.R.:   The Geological Society of Puerto Rico, 1969. 53 p.

Books, reports, journals, extracts and papers with geological chapters or selections are cited alphabetically in this list. Covers Puerto Rico,

Desecheo, Mona, Monito, Culebra, Vieques and surrounding submarine areas. A very useful subject-geographic index adds to the value of this contribution.

2.278.   Leonard, Mortimer. "An Annotated Bibliography of Puerto Rican Entomology." **The Journal of the Department of Agriculture of Puerto Rico** 17 (January 1932): 1-96.

This is an important early bibliography of 711 titles on Puerto Rican entomology and insects. It is organized alphabetically, then chronologically, by author.

2.279.   Martorell, Luis F., Silverio Medina Gaud and Enrique Jordán-Musa. "Indexes to 'The Journal of Agriculture of the University of Puerto Rico' Volumes 1-47 (1917-1963)." **The Journal of Agriculture of the Univerisity of Puerto Rico** 55 (July 1971): 275-357.

Provides bibliographic access to the most influential journal in the field of agriculture, covering the first forty-seven volumes. Cites 993 research reports in the areas of zoology (183), plant pathology (191), agronomy (143), soils and fertilizers (96), chemistry (96), animal husbandry (67), genetics (18), cytology (14), herbicides (11) and the remainder in radiation, statistics, botany, rum chemistry, and other agricultural matters. Complete citations appear under author in the main part. A subject index refers to the appropriate entry numbers. This important contribution was continued in later years by Martorell (2.280), Medina Gaud (2.281), and Vélez (2.308).

2.280.   _____ "Indexes to 'The Journal of Agriculture of the University of Puerto Rico', Volumes 48-52 (1964-1968)." **The Journal of Agriculture of the University of Puerto Rico** 55 (July 1971): 358-85.

This is the first supplement to the previous title. It adds an additional 191 references to the original and also includes a subject index.

2.281.   Medina Gaud, Silverio and Luis F. Martorell. "Indexes to 'The Journal of Agriculture of the University of Puerto Rico', Volumes 53-55 (1969-1971)." **The Journal of Agriculture of the University of Puerto Rico** 55 (October 1971): 520-44.

This second supplement to the original index (2.279) provides another 164 complete bibliographic citations to articles published in **The**

Journal. As in the original work, a subject index increases the usefulness of this publication.

2.282.   Mosquera, Menandra and Jo Anne Feheley. **Bibliography of Forestry in Puerto Rico**. New Orleans, La.:   U.S. Department of Agriculture, Southern Forest Experiment Station, 1984. 196 p. (General Technical Report, SO-51)

Partially annotated. Covers publications on the practice of forestry and related specialties. It is organized alphabetically and has indexes by author, subject and species.

2.283.   Nieves, Luis Oscar. "An Indexed Selected Bibliography of the Ichthyofauna of the Puerto Rico Region: Part 1." **Science-Ciencia: Boletín Científico del Sur** 9 (Winter 1982): 3-20.

Lists "the most important scientific references which include systmatical, biological and ecological data of the marine and fresh-water fishes of the Puerto Rico region." Its 576 entries are arrranged alphabetically by author, followed by an index by families.

2.284.   Ordóñez de Totis, María E. **Bibliografía del café (selectiva)**. Río Piedras, P.R.: Universidad de Puerto Rico, Recinto de Río Piedras, Sistema de Bibliotecas, Bibliotec y Hemeroteca Puertorriqueña, 1983. 57 p.

References to different aspects of coffee and its importance to Puerto Rican life are organized by books, journal articles and photographs.

2.285.   Otero, José I. and Melville T. Cook. "A Bibliography of Mycology and Phytopathology of Central and South America, Mexico and the West Indies." **The Journal of Agriculture of the University of Puerto Rico** 21 (July 1937): 249-86.

Includes many references related to Puerto Rico. Partially annotated.

2.286.   _____ . "El café: bibliografía clasificada y parcialmente anotada." Río Piedras, P.R.: Universidad de Puerto Rico, Estación Experimental Agrícola, 1935. 603 p. (mimeographed)

This exhaustive bibliography on the coffee industry worldwide has numerous references to coffee in Puerto Rico. An important early work which can be supplemented by Ordóñez de Toti's (2.284).

2.287.   Otero, José I. and Melville T. Cook.   "Partial Bibliography of Virus Diseases of Plants." **The Journal of Agriculture of the University of Puerto Rico** 18 (January-April 1934): 5-410.

> Many references to the island situation are made in this general bibliography which is partially annotated. Supplements were published subsequently in **The Journal**: 19 (April 1935): 129-313; 20 (July 1936): 741-818; 22 (July 1938): 263-409.

2.288.   Ortiz Corps, Edgardo.   **An Annotated Checklist of the Recent Marine Gastropoda (Mollusca) from Puerto Rico.** Humacao, P.R.: Colegio Universitario de Humacao, Department of Biology, [1985]. 220 p.

> The checklist describes Puerto Rican molluscs by classes References made in the list are cited completely in the accompanying bibliography. A taxonomic index is appended.

2.289   **Publications of the Mayagüez Institute of Tropical Agriculture.** Mayagüez, P.R.: 1976? 84 p.

> Updates the bibliography prepared by Quirina Rivera Rivera (2.294).

2.290.   Puerto Rico.   Administración de Fomento Económico. **Bibliography of Puerto Rican Geology.** San Juan, P.R.: United States Geological Survey, 1958. 14 p.

> Unannotated list of publications dealing with the geology of the island. The last two pages fall under the heading "Bibliograhy of Paleontological Papers."

2.291.   _____   Departamento de Agricultura. Oficina de Información y Relaciones Públicas. Biblioteca. **Bibliografía del arroz.** Santurce, P.R.: 1979. 9 p.

> Most of the items cited treat some aspect of rice in Puerto Rico: agricultural, comercial, historical and others.

2.292.   "Recent Publications on the Caribbean Area."   **Caribbean Journal of Science** Vol. 1, no. 1, Feruary 1961-

> The journal includedsa bibliography section divided by area of scientific interest (natural sciences). Numerous references to Puerto Rico can be found.

2.293.   Riollano, Arturo. **Contribuciones a la literatura sobre el cultivo y manejo de la caña de azúcar en Puerto Rico.** Río Piedras, P.R.: Estación Experimental Agrícola, Recinto Universitario de Mayagüez, Biblioteca, 1970. 7 p. (Lista bibliográfica, 2)

Ninety-five references to articles, theses and books on sugar cane in Puerto Rico are cited in this publication. Not annotated.

2.294.   Rivera Rivera, Quirina. **Publications of the Federal Experiment Station in Puerto Rico, July 1900 to July 1964.** Mayagüez, P.R.: Federal Experiment Station, 1964? 81 p.

This bibliography of the Station's publications is organized by type of publication: annual reports, bulletins, circulars, agricultural notes, U.S.D.A. miscellaneous publications and articles published in journals and periodicals (arranged by subject). Updated by **Publications of the Mayagüez Institute of Tropical Agriculture**.

2.295.   Rivero, Juan A. and Harold Heatwole. **Herpetogeography of Puerto Rico. VI. A Bibliography of the Herpetology of Puerto Rico and the Virgin Islands.** Washington, D.C.: Division of Reptiles and Amphibians, National Museum of Natural History, 1979. 17 p. (Smithsonian Herpetological Information Service, no. 43)

This list of citations covers all aspects of the island's reptiles and amphibians. Rivero is a highly respected herpetologist at the Mayagüez Campus of the University of Puerto Rico.

2.296.   Sánchez Nieva, F. **Resumen bibliográfico de los trabajos de investigación sobre la utilización de algunas cosechas tropicales llevados a cabo en el Laboratorio de Tecnología de Alimentos, 1951-1979.** Río Piedras, P.R.: Universidad de Puerto Rico, Recinto de Mayagüez, Colegio de Ciencias Agrícolas, Estación Experimental Agrícola, 1980. 69 p. (Publicación 136)

Brief summaries are given of 130 articles on the science and technology of using and consuming various food crops on the island. The bibliography is arranged alphabetically by fruit or vegetable.

2.297.   _____ **An Annotated Bibliography of Tropical Crops Processing Research Conducted at the Food Technology Laboratory, 1951-1979.** Río Piedras, P.R.: 1980. 62 p.

Publication 139 of the University of Puerto Rico's Agricultural Experiment Station. "Summarizes the research in tropical food sciences and technology conducted in Puerto Rico over a period of 30 years." It is organized by crop and subtopics and has a detailed subject index. It was also published in Spanish (2.296).

2.298.   Santiago Blay, Jorge A. "Annotated List of the Scorpion Taxa Reported in Puerto Rico and the Adjacent Islands." **Science-Ciencia: Boletín Científico del Sur** 10 (Summer 1983): 92-93.

The annotated section of this list is organized by the main families of scorpions. It is followed by an alphabetical listing which gives complete bibliographical data.

2.299.   Santiago Vázquez, Antonio et al.   **The Water Resources Situation in Puerto Rico: An Evaluation of Published Information.** Mayagüez, P.R.: School of Engineering, University of Puerto Rico, 1970. 180, 8 p. (WRRI Technical Completion Report, Research Project A-012-PR)

This bibliography of water-related literature is arranged by abstract number. Following each complete citation is a short abstract on the item. Two indexes facilitate access to information: a category index, which uses the categories established by the Committee on Water Resources Research of the Federal Council of Science and Technology, and an author index. A geographical index would also have been useful.

2.300.   Smyth, Graywood. "An Annotated Bibliography of Porto Rican Cane Insects." **The Journal of the Department of Agriculture of Porto Rico** 3 (October 1919): 117-34.

This partially annotated bibliography is arranged chronologically then alphabetically.

2.301.   Soler, Pedro Jaime. "A Bibliography on the Fishes and Fisheries of Puerto Rico." In **Proceedings of the Gulf and Fisheries Institute (3rd: 1950),** edited by C. P. Idyll, 143-49. Coral Gables, Fla.: University of Miami, 1951.

An unannotated list arranged alphabetically by author. Each author's works are cited chronologically. Over 130 references to books, articles, government publications and unpublished materials are described.

2.302.   Steiner, G. and Carmen T. Ramírez. "Bibliography on Agro-and Plant Nematodes of the American Tropics." **The Journal of Agriculture of the University of Puerto Rico** 68 (April 1964): 101-126.

Of the 459 publications mentioned in the bibliography, many refer to parasitic worms found on the island.

2.303.   Stevenson, John A. **Fungi of Puerto Rico and the American Virgin Islands**. Baltimore, Md.:   Reed Herbarium, 1975.   743 p. (Contribution of Reed Herbarium, no. 23)

The bibliography and supplemental references on pages 531 to 578 constitute one of the most complete bibliographies on fungi in Puerto Rico. Over 700 citations are given.

2.304.   Torres, Calixta S.   **Literature Review of Studies on Natural Rum Ageing**. Río Piedras, P.R.: Agricultural Experiment Station, College of Agricultural Sciences, Mayagüez Campus, University of Puerto Rico, 1973. 15 p. (Rum Pilot Plant Project H-263; Report PPR:2-73)

A bibliographic essay on the topic with a final bibliography of fifteen references.

2.305.   Unesco. Centro de Cooperación Científica de la Unesco para América Latina. **Artículos científicos en América Latina, 1950**. Montevideo, Uruguay: 1952. 323 p.

"This volume contains the articles published in Latin America during 1950 , dealing with natural and applied sciences, which have been communicated to this Centre." Articles are arranged by general subjects. The lack of indexes limits the use of this tool. At the front can be found a list of journals and publications of scientific societies of Puerto Rico which are referred to in the book.

2.306.   United States.   Department of Agriculture. Library.   **The Tomato Industry in Puerto Rico and Cuba: A Short List of References**. Washington, D.C.: 194j0. 12 p. (Economic Library Lists, 10)

Although this title was mentioned in an unpublished ACURIL bibliography (1.004), the author was unable to locate a copy for evaluation.

2.307.   Vélez, Manuel J., Jr. "Bibliografía selecta de la fauna y de las comunidades naturales de Puerto Rico." **Science-Ciencia: Boletín Científico del Sur** 6 (Spring 1979): 106-125; 6 (Summer 1979): 145-66.

The first part of this unannotated bibliography covers general aspects, biogeography, and fluvial marine and terrestial communities. The second part gives references to all other aspects related to the island's fauna. Both books and journal articles are included. A useful work in a field not well-served bibliographically.

2.308.   Vélez Delgado, Samuel O., Margaret Inserni and Rosaura Rivera Ostolaza. "Index to 'The Journal of Agriculture of the University of Puerto Rico', Volumes 56-69." **The Journal of Agriculture of the University of Puerto Rico** 69 (October 1985): 457-80.

This is the third supplement to the original index (2.289)). It cites 759 articles and research notes. In the case of co-authors, the senior one is identified with an asterisk. Sole authors are indicated by a dagger ('). Complete citations are also given in the subject index.

2.309.   Wolcott, George N. "Insectae Borinquenses; A Revised Annotated Check-List of the Insects of Puerto Rico." **The Journal of Agriculture of the University of Puerto Rico** 20 (January 1936): 1-600.

An introductory essay, which briefly relates the history of entomology in Puerto Rico to 1935, is followed by a general section of references dealing with several orders. The remainder of the work is organized by order, then family and insect. Illustrated. It is a revision of "'Insectae Portorricensis': A Preliminary Annotated Check-List of the Insects of Porto Rico, with Descriptions of Some New Species", published in **The Journal of the Department of Agriculture of Puerto Rico**, 7 (January 1923): 5-313, and "First Supplement to 'Insectae Portoricensis'", published in the same journal (7 (October 1924): 38-43). Wolcott includes a generic index and a host plant index.

2.310.   _____ "The Insects of Puerto Rico." **The Journal of Agriculture of the University of Puerto Rico** 32 (January-October 1948): 1-975.

This is a complete catalog of the island's insects. As well as a description of each species, all relevant bibliographic references are given. Updates and revises the author's "Insectae Borinquenses" of 1936 (2.309).

SOCIOLOGY AND ANTHROPOLOGY

2.311.   Aldous, Joan and Reuben Hill. **International Bibliogrphy of Research in Marriage and the Family, 1900-1964.** Minneapolis, Minn.: University of Minnesota Press, 1967. 508 p.

Arranged by keyword-in-context, this work includes thirty-two items under "Puerto Rico" and "Puerto Rican." For complete citations one must check each alphameric reference code in the "complete reference list" section.

2.312.   Aponte, Eduardo et al.   **Bibliografía general del niño puertorriqueño: borrador.** Río Piedras, P.R.: Universidad de Puerto Rico, Facultad de Pedagogía, Instituto de Investigaciones del Niño, 1982. 124 p.

A subject-arranged bibliography of journal aritcles and unpublished materials on the Puerto Rican child. It follows the structure of the **Bibliografía de asuntos juveniles en Puerto Rico** (2.327). Symbols represent libraries or agencies having a copy of each item.

2.313.   Aponte Pérez, Francisco. "La criminalidad en Puerto Rico; perfil sociológico-bibliográfico." **Boletín Judicial** 6 (April-June 1984): 6-25.

An historical, bibliographical essay on crime in Puerto Rico. It also includes statistical tables.

2.314.   Behrendt, Richard F. W.   **Modern Latin America in Social Science Literature; A Selected Annotated Bibliography of Books, Pamphlets and Periodicals in English in the Fields of Economics, Politics, and Sociology of Latin America.** Albuquerque, New Mexico: University of New Mexico, 1949. 152 p.

Provides thirty-four entries on Puerto Rico, some of which are anno- tated. Also has chapters on the Caribbean Region and Latin America in general. Author index.

2.315.   "Bibliografía del campesino." **Indice**, 13 January 1930, p.161.

No introduction accompanies this unannotated list of forty-seven references to the Puerto Rican country people ("jíbaro"). Both English and Spanish books and journal articles are cited.

2.316.   Cunningham, Ineke.   "Un inventario de investigaciones relacionadas con cambio social y política oficial en Puerto Rico." **América Indígena** 30 (January 1970): 222-54.

Definitions of social change and official policy set the tone for this bibliographic essay. Following the introduction, the author discusses studies of social change in Puerto Rico, and studies of problems whose solutions will have an impact on both social change and official policy: political status, definition of national culture, economic development, population, education, and social problems. A brief section of conclusions is followed by the detailed bibliography.

2.317.   Delorme, Robert L. **Latin America: Social Science Information Sources, 1967-1979**. Santa Barbara, Calif.: ABC-Clio, 1981. 262 p.

Describes twenty-two books and forty-three journal articles relating to Puerto Rico. Most references are in English.

2.318.   _____. **Latin America, 1979-1983: A Social Science Bibliography**. Santa Barbara, Calif.: ABC-Clio, 1984. 225 p.

Compiled as a sequel to **Latin America: Social Science Information Sources, 1967-1979** (2.317), this bibliography covers Puerto Rico (especially pages 158 to 161). It includes references to books and articles or chapters written in English or Spanish.

2.319.   Earnhardt, Kent C. **Population Research, Policy and Related Studies on Puerto Rico: An Inventory**. Río Piedras, P.R.: Editorial de la Universidad de Puerto Rico, 1984. 132 p.

"The publication represents...an extensive inventory of either published or unpublished but presumably available popultion research, policy, and related studies on Puerto Rico up to and including some entries for 1976." The main section is arranged alphabetically by author. Annotations are fairly lengthy and often consist of quotations from the work cited or from **Population Index**. Classification, indexing and cross-referencing tables provide adequate subject access. An important tool.

2.320.   **Estudios sobre la familia**. San Juan, P.R.: Comisión para la Protección y Fortalecimiento de la Familia en Puerto Rico, Oficina del Gobernador, 1984. 20 p.

Describes studies made at different island universities and by different government agencies. Various factors and problems facing the family are also considered: addiction, deviant behavior, community and personal development, education, health needs, socio-economic problems and bio-social rehabilitation.

2.321.   Levine, Robert M. **Race and Ethnic Relations in Latin America and the Caribbean: An Historical Dictionary and Bibliography**. Metuchen, N.J.: Scarecrow Press, 1980. 252 p.

The index provides access to sixteen references relating to Puerto
Rico. A total of twenty-two items are also cited in the bibliography
section under "Other Caribbean."

2.322.   Mantilla Bazo, Víctor.   **Vivienda y planeamiento en
América Latina: bibliografía preliminar**. Washington, D.C.: Unión
Panamericana, 1952. 112p.

References to housing and planning in Puerto Rico can be found on
pages 68 to 77 of this annotated bibliography. Somewhat dated.

2.323.   Meléndez Muñoz, Miguel. "Bibliografía del jíbaro." In his **Obras
completas**, vol. 3, 465-76. Barcelona, Spain: Ediciones Rumbos, 1963.

This critical essay reviews major nineteenth century literary and
sociological works written on the Puerto Rican "jíbaro." Meléndez, a
distinguished Puerto Rican journalist who studied and wrote about
rural Puerto Rico, points out gaps in the literature as well as major
works and characteristics. This work was also published as
"Bibliografía del jíbaro en el siglo XIX" in **Puerto Rico Ilustrado**, 17
April, 1941, pp. 14-16.

2.324.   Miranda, Altagracia.   **Fuentes puertorriqueñas de
referencia en las ciencias sociales**.   San Juan, P.R.:   Sociedad de
Bibliotecarios de Puerto Rico, 1975. 14 p. (Cuadernos bibliotecológicos,
11)

A selection of important Puerto Rican reference books in the field of
the social sciences is described under the following headings:
bibliographies, biography, dictionaries, directories and manuals. No
new edition has been published.

2.325.   Pantel, A. Gus. "Bibliografía de antropología física en el
Caribe."   **Boletín   Informativo   Fundación   Arqueológica,
Antropológica e Histórica de Puerto Rico** 3 (December 1977): 1-9.

References to Puerto Rico may be found in this unannotated list which
is divided into two sections: prehistoric populations and contemporary populations. The user would be well advised to consult Sued
Badillo's work as well (2.331).

2.326.   Poblete Troncoso, Moisés. **Ensayo de bibliografía social de
los países hispano-americanos**. Santiago, Chile: 1936. 210 p.

Vicente Géigel Polanco contributed to the section on Puerto Rico. There is no apparent order to the fifty-eight unannotated entries for different materials dealing with the social sciences on the island.

2.327.   Puerto Rico. Oficina del Coordinador de Asuntos Juveniles. **Bibliografía de asuntos juveniles en Puerto Rico: índice de publicaciones hechas sobre este tema en y fuera de Puerto Rico durante los años 1945 al 1965.** San Juan, P.R.: 1966. 158 p.

Entries appear alphabetically under the following topics: delinquency; education; family; institutions; miscellaneous; recreation, religion, health (mental, physical and social); and work. Libraries having a copy of each item are indicated. Some entries include a brief summary of contents. The lack of an index tends to reduce the bibliography's usefulness.

2.328.   Ríos, Luis F. **Bibliografía selectiva sobre la pobreza en Puerto Rico desde 1940-1982.** Arecibo, P.R.: Universidad de Puerto Rico, Administración de Colegios Regionales, Colegio Universitario Tecnológico de Arecibo, Biblioteca, 1985. 15 p.

Focuses on references to the health, economic, political and educational aspects of poverty on the island from 1940 to 1982. Refers only to material owned by the library.

2.329.   Seda de Rodríguez, Rita M. **La familia puertorriqueña: bibliografía selectiva.** Mayagüez, P.R.: Universidad de Puerto Rico, Recinto Universitario de Mayagüez, Biblioteca, 1985. 20 p. **Suplemento.** 1986. 13 p. (Serie de bibliografías ocasionales, 11, 11A)

Materials on the Puerto Rican family are identified in four sections: books, newspaper articles, journals and government documents. No annotations are provided. All items can be found in the library.

2.330.   **Sociologie de la famille antillaise: bibliographie analytique.** Montreal, Quebec: Centre de Recherches Caraibes, Université de Montreal, 1977. 86 p.

An annotated bibliography in French on the family in Caribbean countries, including Puerto Rico (pages 64 to 72). Most of the citations are for English-language sources.

2.331.   Sued Badillo, Jalil. **Bibliografía antropológica para el estudio de los pueblos indígenas en el Caribe.** Santo Domingo: Fundacíon García-Arévalo, 1977. 579 p.

Useful, unannotated bibliography consisting of two main parts: subjects and areas. The topics covered in the former are: general works; archaeological sources; ethnographic sources; geographic sources; historical sources; and linguistics sources. Some references to Puerto Rico can be found in these sections. However, most such references are located in the part on areas, under Puerto Rico. Each part is arranged alphabetically by author. When more than one entry appears under the author's name these are arranged chronologically. No general index.

2.332.   Toro Calder, Jaime. "Bibliografía sobre delincuencia juvenil." **Revista de Derechos Humanos** 4 (October 1973): 77-83.

Unannotated bibliography of 122 references to books, journal articles, reports, theses and government documents.

2.333.   _____ **Bibliografía sobre delincuencia juvenil en Puerto Rico.** Río Piedras, P.R.: Centro de Investigaciones Sociales, Universidad de Puerto Rico, 1974. 15 p.

An alphabetical list of books, journal articles, theses and government publications.

2.334.   _____ **Bibliografía sobre sociología de la desviación social y glosario criminológico: Puerto Rico 1971.** Río Piedras, P.R.: Centro de Investigaciones Sociales, Facultad de Ciencias Sociales, Recinto de Río Piedras, Universidad de Puerto Rico, 1971. 63 p.

The bibliography section is arranged alphabetically under these topics: adult delinquency, juvenile delinquency, drug addiction, alcoholism and others. Covers books, aritcles, reports and theses.

2.335.   United States.   National Institute of Mental Health. **Bibliography on Racism.** Washington, D.C.: 1972-

Volume one covers up to 1971. The second volume, published in 1978, cites materials published from 1972 to 1975. All items deal with racism and mental health. Those which focus on Puerto Ricans can be found by consulting the subject index. Volume two has a complete section on Hispanics where other relevant materials can be found. Helpful abstracts clarify the subject matter and scope of each entry.

2.336.   Universidad de Puerto Rico. Centro de Investigaciones Sociales. "Bibliografía acumulativa." In its **Informe anual 1984-85,** 91-132. Río Piedras, P.R.: 1985?

An alphabetical listing of publications relating to Puerto Rico, in terms of the social sciences. It is divided by books and by monographs, pamplets and articles. Most annual reports published by the Center cite materials published during the year. The 1956-1957 annual report had an important cumulative bibliography which covered from 1930 to 1954. The latter was contributed by María O'Neill López.

2.337.   Universidad de Puerto Rico.   Centro de Investigaciones Pedagógicas. **Bibliografía anotada de artículos acerca de la juventud**. Río Piedras, P.R.: Universidad de Puerto Rico, 1971. 143 p. (Monografías del Centro de Investigaciones Pedagógicas. Serie A, 1)

This annotated bibliography covers Puerto Rican newspaper articles published from 1960 to 1971 on the island's youth. It is arranged by topic with an author index.

2.338.   _____. Escuela Graduada de Trabajo Social. **Lista de tesis de la Escuela Graduada de Trabajo Social, Beatriz Lassalle de la Universidad de Puerto Rico desde 1945 hasta 1970.** Río Piedras, P.R.: 1971. 18 p.

Arranged chronologically, then alphabetically under each year. Some annual lists have been published to update this unannotated list.

2.339.   _____   _____. Biblioteca. "Bibliografía selectiva sobre alcoholismo." Río Piedras, P.R.: 1973. 16 p. (mimeographed)

A general bibligraphy on alcoholism which includes many references to the problem in Puerto Rico. This work was also published as part of the Library's **Problemas sociales: una guía selectiva** (2.340).

2.340.   _____   _____.   _____. "Problemas sociales: una guía selectiva." Río Piedras, P.R.: 1974. 41 p. (mimeographed)

A collection of general bibliographies on alcoholism, abortion, drug addiction, discrimination and minorities, manpower and violence. The bibliography on alcoholism has many references related to the problem in Puerto Rico, especially newspaper articles. This part was also issued separtely (2.339). Fewer references to Puerto Rico can be found in the bibliography on racism.

2.341.   University of North Carolina.   Carolina Population Center. Technical Information Service. "PopScan Bibliography No. 180: Puerto Rico." Chapel Hill, N.C.: University of North Carolina, Carolina Population Center, 1976. 14 p.

This is a computer-produced list of materials owned by the Center's Library. It covers population, family planning and demography. It is cited in Earnhardt (2.319), but was not examined by the author.

2.342.   University of Texas.   Department of Sociology.   Population Research Center. **International Population Census Bibliography: Latin America and the Caribbean.** Austin, Tex.: Bureau of Business Research, University of Texas, 1965. 1 vol. (Census Bibliography, no. 1)

The section on the census publications on Puerto Rico is arranged chronologically from 1765 to 1960. Not annotated. An updated version would be helpful.

2.343.   Vaughan, Denton R. **Urbanization in Twentieth Century Latin America: A Working Bibliography.** Austin, Tex.: Institute of Latin American Studies, Population Research Center, 1973. 122 p.

Emphasizes journal literature from 1965 to 1969 and is arranged geographically. The Puerto Rican section can be found on pages 86 to 88. Both English and Spanish articles can be found among the twenty-eight citations corresponding to urbaization on the island.

WOMEN

2.344.   Alicea de Vázquez, Aida.   "La mujer en Puerto Rico: bibliografía." **Homines** 10 (July 1986-February 1987): 511-15.

This unannotated bibliography appears to be reproduced from a bibliography prepared for the General Library at the University of Puerto Rico. It is organized in three sections: books, journal articles and miscellaneous materials.

2.345.   Azize, Yamila. "Bibliogrfía de libros sobre la mujer en Puerto Rico." **Homines** 10 (July 1986-February 1987): 516-23.

Taken from one of the compiler's books (**La mujer en la lucha.** San Juan, P.R.: Editorial Cultural, 1985), this bibliography lists books, journals, newspapers, articles and other materials on the Puerto Rican woman. It is one of the most complete available but unfortunately it is not annotated.

2.346.   "Bibliografía selecta: la mujer en la historia y cultura puertorriqueña." **Redes de Comunicación** 4 (1982?): [1-14]

This is a reprint of a bibliography included in "Social Studies and History Supplements: Contributions of Women; Final Report to the Women's Educational Equity Act Program, Commission for the Improvement of Women's Rights". Isabel Picó was the Project Director. The report was written in June of 1979. No annotations are given.

2.347.   Cortina, Lynn Ellen Price.   **Spanish-American Women Writers: A Bibliographical Research Checklist.** New York: Garland Publishing, Inc., 1983. 292 p.

Of uneven quality. The main purpose of the book is to identify Spanish American women writers. Puerto Rico's women authors are listed on pages 225 to 243. The information given varies, often consisting only of the author's name. In other cases the title and dates of the works are also given, as are pseudonyms.

2.348.   Corvalán, Graciela N. V. **Latin American Women Writers in English Translation: A Bibliography.** Los Angeles, Calif.:   Latin American Studies Center, California State University, 1980. 109 p.

Some Puerto Rican women authors are included in this alphabetically arranged work. Nationalities and birth and death dates are indicated for each entry. If the work appears in anthologies, this fact is indicated by the corresponding abbreviation and page numbers. Critical works are listed after the author's works which are cited by genre.

2.349.   Cotera, Martha.   **Multicultural Women's Sourcebook: Materials Guide   for   Use   in   Women's   Studies   and Bilingual/Multicultural Programs.** Edited by Nella Cunningham. Washington, D.C.: Women's Educational Equity Act Program, U.S. Department of Education, 1982. 167 p. (ED 216 234)

Brief annotations describe the thirty-eight references to Puerto Rican women, seventeen of which are identified as appropriate for school students. Covers books, journals and theses.

2.350.   Delgado Cintrón, Carmelo. "Propuesta para un curso sobre los derechos de la mujer: esquema de estudios y guía bibliográfico." **Revista del Colegio de Abogados de Puerto Rico** 45 (January-December 1984): 95-107.

An important bibliography on women and their rights. Most of the seventy-five references deal specifically with the Puerto Rican woman. A proposed course outline on women is also sketched.

2.351.   Instituto Interamericano de Ciéncias Agrícolas.   Centro Interamericano de Documentación e Información Agrícola. **Bibliografía: participación de la mujer en el desarrollo rural de América Latina y el Caribe.** San José, Costa Rica: 1980. 103 p. (Serie documentación e información agrícola, 78)

> An unannotated bibliography on woman's role in the rural development of Latin America and the Caribbean. It is organized by subject and has an author index. The lack of a geographical index hampers the identification of materials dealing with a particular country such as Puerto Rico.

2.352.   Knaster, Meri. **Women in Spanish America: An Annotated Bibliography from Pre-Conquest to Contemporary Times.** Boston: G. K. Hall, 1977. 696 p.

> An extensive, annotated bibliography that is arranged by major sub-jects. Each topic is subdivided geographically with entries for Puerto Rico appearing under the heading Caribbean. Approximately 119 citations refer to Puerto Rican women. Author and subject indexes are included.

2.353.   López de Díaz, Aura. **Bibliografía de la mujer: textos de historia, antropología, sociología, política, medios de comunicación y otros aspectos de la mujer como ser social, que se encuentra en el Sistema de Bibliotecas de la Universidad de Puerto Rico.** Río Piedras, P.R.: Biblioteca, Escuela de Comunicación Pública, Departamento de Bibliotecas Graduadas, Universidad de Puerto Rico, Recinto de Río Piedras, 1983. 56 p.

> A general bibliography on women with a special part on Puerto Ricans (pages 48 to 56). This section is subdivided into the following topics: general aspects, biography, historical evolution, social conditions, employment, women's rights, legislation, discrimination, suffrage and women in literature. A laudable contribution and finding tool.

2.354.   Marting, Diane E., ed. **Women Writers of Spanish America: An Annotated Bio-Bibliographical Guide.** New York: Greenwood Press, 1987. 448 p.

> Only nineteen of the seventy entries for Puerto Rico have biographical information and annotations for works cited. The other entries include only birth and death dates where known, and a list of titles which are by no means exhaustive. The authors of the annotations can be identified by their initials.

2.355.   Stuart, Bertie A. **Women in the Caribbean: A Bibliography**. Leiden, Netherlands: Department of Caribbean Studies, Royal Institutue of Linguistics and Anthropology, 1979. 163 p.

> This annotated work is arranged by subject with indexes by author and category. Entries for materials dealing with the Puerto Rican woman are identified by the abbreviation "PR" in the left-hand margin. Books, journals and proceedings are included. The indexes add to the value of the book.

OTHERS

2.356.   Corro, Alejandro del. **Puerto Rico: obispos nativos, 1962-65; documentos y reacciones de prensa**. Cuernavaca, Mexico: Centro Intercultural de Documentación, 1967. 1 vol. (various pagings) (CIDOC Dossier, 16)

> The first part of this book is a bibliography on a controversy that arose as to whether or not Puerto Ricans should be raised to the office of bishop of the Catholic Church. It is presented chronologi-cally in five sections: 1951 to July 29, 1962; August 6, 1962 to January 1963; April 22, 1963 to October 22, 1964; November 5, 1964 to March 7, 1965; and March 29 to October 21, 1965. In the second part of the book the author reproduces a great many of the articles mentioned in the bibliography. An author-subject index is included.

2.357.   González Padró, Pedro. **Fuentes puertorriqueñas de referencia en el área de las humanidades**. San Juan, P.R.: Sociedad de Bibliotecarios de Puerto Rico, 1974. 25 p. (Cuadernos bibliotecológicos, 7)

> Annotated references and lists of relevant journals are given for each of the following areas of the humanities: fine arts, philosophy, linguistics and literature and religion.

2.358.   Inter American Statistical Institute. **Bibliography of Selected Statistical Sources of the American Nations. Bibliografía de fuentes estadísticas escogidas de las naciones americanas**. Washington, D.C.: Inter American Statistical Institute, 1947. 689 p.

> Includes thirteen references to Puerto Rico (pages 287 to 288). This publication was kept up to date by **Estadística**, a journal of the American Statistical Institute.

2.359.   Lent, John A. **Caribbean Mass Communications: A Comprehensive Bibliography**. Waltham, Ma.: Crossroads Press, 1981. 152p.

Sponsored by the African Studies Association, this book includes sixty-one specific references to mass communications in Puerto Rico.

2.360.   Martínez de Hernández, Tomasita. **Fuentes estadísticas sobre Puerto Rico: bibliografía selectiva anotada e índice a la "Revista Estadística"**. Mayagüez, P.R.: Universidad de Puerto Rico, Recinto Universitario de Mayagüez, Biblioteca, Centro de Datos Censales, 1985. 14 p.

Covers publications from 1980 to 1984 that supplement and update federal censuses. An annotated title index of aritcles in the **Revista Estadística** is also included.

2.361.   Mundo Lo, Sara de. **Index to Spanish American Collective Biography**. Vol. 3. **The Central American and Caribbean Countries**. Boston: G. K. Hall, 1984.

Constitutes a good bibliography of biographical sources, both general and specialized. Following each bibliographical entry is either a description of the information covered or a list of biographees.

2.362.   Ortiz Guerra, Miguel Angel. **Conferencia '86:   las humanidades en el Puerto Rico de hoy: una bibliografía selectiva**. Mayagüez, P.R.:   Recinto Universitario de Mayagüez y Fundación Puertorriqueña de las Humanidades, 1986. 53 p.

Organized by subjects and subtopics, this work is basically unanno-tated although some explanatory notes are given for some entries. It is a fairly comprehensive compilation which may be consulted in con-junction with a similar list prepared by Zacarías and Seda (2.367).

2.363.   Sánchez, Nílda. **¿Amenaza nuclear en Puerto Rico?** Bayamón, P.R.: Centro de Recursos del Aprendizaje, Colegio Universitario Tecnológico de Bayamón, Universidad de Puerto Rico, 1985. 19 p.

An unannotated bibliography on the threat of nuclear arms and war to Puerto Rico. The references are presented in four sections: general aspects, political and legal aspects, biological and psychological as-pects, and ethical and religious aspects. Abbreviations are used to indicate libraries or institutions where the items can be found.

2.364.   Schon, Isabel. **A Hispanic Heritage: A Guide to Juvenile Books about Hispanic People and Cultures**. Metuchen, N.J.: Scarecrow Press, Inc., 1980. 168 p.

> This work is designed as an aid for librarians and teachers who are interested in exposing students to the cultures of Hispanic people through books for children and adolescents. Materials on Puerto Ricans can be found on pages 97 to 124 and are organized alphabetically by author. Complete bibliographic citations are accompanied by annotations and an indication of grade level.

2.365.   Toro, Josefina del. "A Bibliography of the Collective Biography of Spanish America." **The University of Puerto Rico Bulletin** 9th ser. 1 (September 1938): 1-140.

> On pages 61 to 72 can be found sources of Puerto Rican collective biography. Complete bibliographical citations are followed by a list of biographees included in each work. This source would have been made more useful by the inclusion of a general index of biographees.

2.366.   Woods, Richard D. **Reference Materials on Latin America in English: The Humanities**. Metuchen, N.J.: Scarecrow Press, 1980. 639 p.

> A valuable, annotated bibliography of about 1200 reference books on Latin America, almost all of which were published in English. Although the arrangement is alphabetical by author, materials concerned with Puerto Rico can be located by using the subject index. Locations for most items are given.

2.367.   Zacarías, Esthervinda and Rita M. Seda. **Las humanidades en Puerto Rico: bibliografía**. Mayagüez, P.R.: Universidad de Puerto Rico, Recinto Universitario de Mayagüez, 1986. 88 p. (Serie de bibliografías ocasionales, 13)

> Organized in three main sections: books, arranged by discipline, then alphabetically by author; newspaper articles; and journals. The latter is a list of magazines in the field of humanities with and author index to the journal **Cuadernos de la Facultad de Humanidades** (U.P.R.). See also a similar bibliography by Ortiz Guerra (2.362).

Puerto Ricans in the United States

3.001.   Arnold, Bill R. and Susan B. Hancock. **The Hispanic Handi-capped: A Bibliographic Listing of Relevant Attitudinal Research.** N.p.: 1982. 21 p. (ED 235 636)

Covers 215 journal articles and dissertation abstracts related to the following topics: employer attitudes; family-relative attitudes; attitudes of the Hispanic hadicapped; rehabilitation service provider attitudes. Articles for Puerto Ricans in the United States must be searched for one-by-one as there is no general index.

3.002.   "A Bibliography on the Puerto Rican Population and Selected Background Studies." **IRCD Bulletin** 4 (January 1968): 9-12.

Only English-language sources are cited. References are divided into four sections: island background; Puerto Rican migrants in the United States; bibliographies (four entries); and reviews of Oscar Lewis's controversial study, **La Vida.** (Also reprinted in **The Puerto Ricans: Migration and General Bibliography.** New York: Arno Press, 1975)

3.003.   Biddle, Stanton F. "Puerto Rican New Yorkers: A Guide to Available Materials at the Municipal Reference Library." **Municipal Reference Library Notes** (New York Public Library) 41 (September 1967): 81-87.

A "...selected list of [eighty-five] publications on New Yorkers of Puerto Rican birth or extraction and their problems. The list includes publicly and privately financed studies, research projects, census data, official reports, and some writings by interested individuals."

3.004.   Bobson, Sarah. **The Education of Puerto Ricans on the Mainland: An Annotated Bibliography.** New York: ERIC Clearinghouse

on Urban Education, Institute for Urban and Minority Education, 1975. 81 p.
(ERIC-CUE Urban Disadvantaged Series, no. 42) (ED 110 586)

The 442 documents covered are "directed to educators concerned with
meeting the critical pedagogical needs of children and youth from
this ethnic minority." The work is organized in the following
sections: general information; historical perspective/background
information on Puerto Rico; inservice education/inservice workshops;
Puerto Ricans and the schools; sociological analysis; Spanish-
language texts; and bibliographies. Only information in the ERIC
collection and the local ERIC collection at Teachers College is cited.
Author index included.

3.005.   Brana-Shute, Rosemary, comp. **A Bibliography of Caribbean
Migration and Caribbean Immigrant Communities.**   With the
assistance of Rosemariin Hoefte.   Gainesville, Fla.:   Reference and
Bibliographic Department, University of Florida Libraries in cooperation
with the Center for Latin American Studies, University of Florida, 1983.
339 p. (Bibliographic series, no. 9)

An important, selective, interdisciplinary bibliography of published
and unpublished materials. Although it is organized alphabetically by
author, the appendices provide for access by topic and geographic
areas. For example, by looking under Puerto Rico in Appendix D,
"Origin of Migrants," pertinent citations can be found. References to
return migration appear under Pueto Rico in Appendix E, "Destinations
of Migrants." Appendix F is a topical index in which such headings as
bibliographies can be searched for related entries. This is one of the
most useful bibliographies of recent years on migration and return
migration. It may be used in conjunction with works by Carrasquillo
(3.010). and Vivó (3.060).

3.006.   Caliguri, Joseph P., Jack P. Krueger and Young Pei.   **An
Annotated Bibliographical Guide to the Literature on Bilingualism
and Multicultural Education.** Kansas City: University of Missouri, 1980.
203 p. (ED 205 365)

Although it emphasizes works written from 1975 to 1980, this guide
covers 1963 to 1980. The introduction traces the changing importance and issues of bilingual and bicultural education. Each of the four
major sections has its own table of contents: bilingualism and elementary education; multiculturalism and secondary education; multiculturalism and higher education; related topics. The lack of an index
makes it difficult to locate the numerous references to Puerto Ricans.
However, this is an important contribution.

3.007.   Camarillo, Albert, ed. **Latinos in the United States: A Bibliography**. Santa Barbara, Calif.: ABC-CLIO, 1986. 332 p.

"This bibliography contains 1382 citations expertly drawn from dozens of volumes of **America: History and Life** published between 1973 and 1985." As well as general works, it includes numerous references to Puerto Rico and Puerto Ricans in the United States. These are easily located in the subject index. The book is organized in the following way: historiography, bibliography, and an overview; colonization and settlement, up to 1848; people from Mexico; people from the Caribbean, Central America, and South America. Annotations are of varying lengths.

3.008.   Cardona, Luis A. **An Annotated Bibliography on Puerto Rican Materials and Other Sundry Matters**. Bethseda, Md.: Carreta Press, 1983. 156 p.

Entries are arranged by their format: books; government documents and reports; conferences, reports and studies; journals; material in the National Archives of the United States; and oral history. Indexes by author, title and subject facilitate access to the annotated entries. Meant to emphasize Puerto Ricans in the United States, the book also studies basic sources that are important in obtaining understanding of Puerto Rico's history and reality in general.

3.009.   _____. **A Selected Directory of Audio Visual Materials on Puerto Rico and the Puerto Ricans**. With a foreword by Antonio Pantoja. Bethseda, Md.: Carreta Press, 1984. 56 p.

The main part of this work lists 120 motion pictures and fifty-five filmstrips which deal with Puerto Rico and Puerto Ricans in the United States. Short content descriptions accompany the entries. Indexes are by subject and title. A list of film libraries is also included.

3.010.   Carrasquillo, Angela L. and Ceferino Carrasquillo. **Annotated Bibliography on Return Migration to Puerto Rico**. N.p.: 1985. 23 p. (ED 261 111)

In their introduction the authors briefly trace the history of Puerto Rican migrations to and from the mainland as well as defining the term return migration. The annotated bibliography consists of sixty-three alphabetically-arranged items: books, articles, theses and government publications. Most of the entries are for English-language sources. Useful annotations. Compare with Brana-Shute's compilation (3.005) and Vivó's (3.060).

3.011.   **Cartel: Annotated Bibliography of Bilingual Biculutural Materials**. Austin, Tex.: Dissemination Center for Bilingual Bicultural Education, 1974. (ED 126 730)

This was a cumulative edition of the Center's publication **Cartel**. It includes Puerto Rican materials available on the mainland. Brief annotations supplement the bibliographic information.

3.012.   City University of New York. Hunter College. Centro de Estudios Puertorriqueños. **Microfilm Holdings**. New York: Evelina López Antonetty Puerto Rican Research Collection, Centro de Estudios Puertorriqueños, Hunter College, City University of New York, 1986. 29 p.

Reflects the library's holdings of nineteenth and twentieth century periodicals. For each title the following information is provided: place of publication, director(s), frequency, type of publication, intended audience and holdings. Other sections included are: scattered issues on one reel, working class newspapers and documents.

3.013.   _____. _____. _____ **Preliminary Guide to Articles in 'La Prensa' Relating to Puerto Ricans in New York City between 1922 and 1929**. New York: 1981. 68 p.

Describes articles from **La Prensa** for the period indicated. The guide is arranged chronologically. Covers all aspects of the Puerto Rican experience in the city. No subject index.

3.014.   _____. _____. _____. History Task Force. **Sources for the Study of Puerto Rican Migration, 1879-1930.** New York: 1982. 224 p.

This is something more than a bibliography. In addition to full bibliographic citations, documents are reproduced, much like an anthology. It is organized chronologically.

3.015.   Condon, E. C. **Bibliography on Migrants and Migrant Education**. New Brunswick, N.J.: Rutgers University, 1982. 47 p. (ED 238 598)

A small section of seven references deals specifically with Puerto Ricans. However, helpful general references can be found in other general sections such as children, economics, education, family,

health and others. Covers from 1970 to 1980. Materials cited can be
found in the Rutgers Inter Cultural Relations and Ethnic Studies
Institute.

3.016.   Cordasco, Francesco et al. **The Equality of Educational
Opportunity: A Bibliography of Selected References**. Totowa, N.J.:
Littlefield, Adams & Co., 1973. 139 p.

One of the essays, "Puerto Ricans on the Mainland: The Educational
Experience", is followed by a selective, annotated bibliography
arranged under three headings: general bibliographies, general
studies, and education. Includes thirty-three references. This source
is still cited frequently.

3.017.   _____ **Immigrant Children in American Schools: A
Classified and Annotated Bibliography with Selected Source
Documents**. Fairfield, N.J.: Augustus M. Kelley Publishers, 1976. 1 vol.

This selective bibliography traces the immigrant child's experiences
in American schools. References to Puerto Rican children can be
found by consulting the index which supplements the work.

3.018.   _____ **The People of Puerto Rico; A Bibliography**.
New York: 1968. 45 p.

No introduction accompanies this unannotated list of materials on
Puerto Ricans in the United States. Most of the publications cited
deal with New York and most, but not all, are in English. (Also
reprinted in **The Puerto Ricans: Migration and General
Bibliography**. New York: Arno Press, 1975.)

3.019.   _____, Eugene Bucchioni and Diego Castellanos. **Puerto
Ricans on the United States Mainland: A Bibliography of Reports,
Texts, Critical Studies and Related Materials**. Totowa, N.J.: Rowman
and Littlefield, 1972. 146 p.

A partially annotated bibliography. The introduction presents the
"Puerto Rican experience on the mainland as it occurs in the schools,
the most sensitive of social institutions." The work is organized into
six main parts: general bibliographies; the island experience; the
migration to the mainland; the mainland experience; the mainland
experience--education; and the mainland experience--the social
context. An author index is included.

3.020.   Cordasco, Francesco and Leonard Covello. "Studies of Puerto Rican Children in American Schools: A Preliminary Bibliography." **Journal of Human Relations** 16 (Second quarter 1968): 264-85.

   The compilers felt that annotations were unnecessary since "the individual titles are generally a clear indication of concern." Following an introduction and a brief list of bibliographical material, the bibliography is arranged in three main sections: unpublished materials (most of which belong to Covello); published materials; published and unpublished material of the New York City Board of Education. (Also reprinted in **The Puerto Ricans: Migration and General Bibliography.** New York: Arno Press, 1975)

3.021.   Darabi, Katherine. **Childbearing among Hispanics in the United States: An Annotated Bibliography.** New York: Greenwood Press, 1987. 167 p.

   Of the 364 annotations which make up this work, approximately eighty-seven deal specifically with Puerto Ricans in the United States. The book covers fertility determinants, pregnancy and fertility, fertility regulation, consequences of childbearing, and some general topics. Titles which consider adolescent pregnancy are identified by an asterisk before the author's name. Author and title indexes appended.

3.022.   Duran, Daniel Flores, et al. **A Bilingual and Bicultural Annotated List of Print and Multimedia Resources for the Puerto Rican Child, Grades K-6.** Madison, Wis.: State Department of Public Instruction, Office of Equal Education Opportunities, 1977. 24 p. (ED 177 868)

   Cites and describes materials appropriate for the bilingual and bicultural education of Puerto Rican children from kindergarten through the sixth grade. As well as print and nonprint resources, it includes references to professional aids.

3.023.   _____. **Latino Materials: A Multimedia Guide for Children and Young Adults.** New York: Neal Schuman, 1979. 249 p.

   "Intended for the librarian, teacher, and curriculum specialist concerned with identifying and selecting materials for programs on both the elementary and secondary levels, and for professional use." Also serves as a guide for selection. Critical annotations are provided for general Latino resources and on Puerto Rican resources in particular. The section on Puerto Rico is divided by elementary, secondary and professional materials. Includes books, journals and films. A glossary and indexes conclude the book.

3.024.   Falcón, Angelo. "Bibliographic Essay: An Introduction to the Literature of Puerto Rican Politics in Urban America." In **Puerto Rican Politics in Urban America**, edited by James Jennings and Monte Rivera, 145-54. Westport, Conn.: Greenwood Press, 1984.

"This essay is a chronological introduction to this literature and does not attmept an analysis of the many issues it raises." Describes sociological studies, works on the nationalist movement, disserta- tions and others. Falcón points out the absence of an authoritative general history of Puerto Rican politics in the United States.

3.025.   Giese, James and Milton J. Gold. **Multicultural Education: A Functional Bibliography for Teachers**. Omaha, Nebr.: Teachers Corps, Center for Urban Education, The University of Nebraska, 1977. 46 p. (ED 143 563)

Two general sections precede the sections on specific ethnic groups: multicultural materials, and prejudice and discrimination. The section on Puerto Ricans cites books and journals that illustrate or discuss the Puerto Rican experience. Some items are curriculum guides or aids for teachers. All references are to English-language sources.

3.026.   Gilmore, Dolores D. and Kenneth Petrie. **People: Annotated Multiethnic Bibliography K-12**. Rockville, Md.:   Montgomery County Public School, 1973. 345 p. (ED 099 864)

Meant to serve educators, this bibliography has many English-language sources on Puerto Rico and Puerto Ricans under the following sub- headings: on island; on mainland; customs, folklore, literature, music; biography; fiction; periodicals (two); and sources and resources. Grade level is indicated where appropriate.

3.027.   Goldberg, Gertrude S. "Puerto Rican Migrants on the Mainland of the United States: A Review of the Literature." **IRCD Bulletin** 4 (January 1968): 1-6.

Sources cited in this bibliographic essay are intended to help one understand the Puerto Rican in the United States. All materials in- cluded are in English, with emphasis on social science materials. A brief section on the island background appears at the beginning of the essay. (Also reprinted in **The Puerto Ricans: Migration and General Bibliography.** New York: Arno Press, 1975.)

3.028.   Herrera, Diane. **Puerto Ricans and Other Minority Groups in the Continental United States; An Annotated Bibliography.** With a new foreword and supplemental bibliography by Francesco Cordasco. Detroit: Blaine Ethridge, 1977. xxi, 397 p.

> Initially published as **Puerto Ricans in the United States: A Review of the Literature** (3.029). In addition to Cordasco's supplementary bibliography, the book has four main parts: bibliographies; the Puerto Rican child in the American system; the Puerto Rican experience on the mainland, and unpublished materials. Author index.

3.029   _____ **Puerto Ricans in the United States: A Review of the Literature.** Austin, Tex.: Dissemination Center for Bilingual Bicultural Education, 1973. 398 p.. (ED 108 488)

> Originally intended as a review of the literature on the educational experience of mainland Puerto Rican children, the scope of the bibliography was expanded to include items of historical, economic, sociological and anthropological relevance to the mainland experience. It includes some materials on other minority groups, especially in areas where little or no specific research on Puerto Ricans has yet been done. Four main divisions make up the main body of the work: bibliographies; the Puerto Rican child in the American educational system; the Puerto Rican experience on the mainland; and unpublished materials. Author index.

3.030.   **Hispanic Americans in the United States: A Selected Bibliography, 1963-1974.** Washington, D.C.: U.S. Dept. of Housing and Urban Development, 1974. 28 p. (ED 096 089)

> Includes a section of fifty-six items on Puerto Ricans and other Caribbean Spanish-speaking peoples. The unannotated list covers English-language books, reports, articles and bibliographies which provide "general historical background and insights into...educational, economic and social adjustment"   References in the general section may yield some additional information on Puerto Ricans.

3.031.   Jablonsky, Adelaide.   **The Education of Puerto Rican Children and Youth: An Annotated Bibliography of Doctoral Dissertations.** With the technical assistance of Jean Barabas. New York: ERIC Information Retrieval Center on the Disadvantaged, Institute for Urban

and Minority Education, Teachers College, Columbia University, 1974. 33 p.
(ED 094 054) (ERIC/IRCD Doctoral Research Series, 6)

Arranged chronoligically from 1965 to 1973 under three main topics:
studies of Puerto Rican students on the mainland; comparisons of
Puerto Rican students with other ethnic groups; and studies of
schools and students in Puerto Rico. Each of the twenty-two entries
includes a full bibliographic citation and a lengthy annotation which
summarizes the dissertation. Indexes by subject, author and
institution.

3.032.   Jakle, John A. **Ethnic and Racial Minorities in North
America: A Selected Bibliography of the Geographical Literature.**
With the assistance of Cynthia A. Jakle. Monticello, Ill.: Council of Planning
Librarians, 1973. 73 p. (ED 134 670)

Citations refer to studies of minorities from the point of view of
geographers, planners and other social scientists. Ten entries deal
mainly with the Puerto Rican migrant's choice of location in the
United States.

3.033.   Jenkins, Shirley and Barbara Morrison. **Ethnicity and Child
Welfare: An Annotated Bibliography.** New York: Columbia University
School of Social Work, 1974. 47 p. (ED 139 875)

Puerto Ricans are one of the five groups covered in this list of
materials published from 1963 to 1973 in books, journals, papers and
other sources. Materials cited relate to child welfare as affected by
ethnic origins. The section on Puerto Ricans has twenty-five
references, all in English. A small section of general references is
included and might yield additional information.

3.034.   Johnson, Harry, A., ed. **Ethnic American Minorities: A
Guide to Media and Materials.** New York: R.R. Bowker, 1976. 304 p.

Entries on Puerto Rico and Puerto Ricans in the United States are
included in the section "The Spanish-speaking American," written by
Lourdes Miranda King. The annotated entries indicate format, grade
level, release date if known, and other details such as duration. The
subject index helps provide direct access to the titles.

3.035.   Kinton, Jack F. **American Ethnic Groups and the Revival
of Cultural Pluralism: Evaluative Sourcebook for the 1970's.** 4th
ed. Aurora, Ill.: Social Science & Sociological Resources, 1974. 206 p.

Cover title: **American Ethnic Groups: A Sourcebook**. The main
section on Puerto Ricans in America can be found on pages 102 to 106.
Bibliographic references are given for fifty-one books, and twenty-
seven journal articles. Some of the items included give background
information on Puerto Ricans and do not necessarily deal with Puerto
Ricans on the mainland. Examples of these are Gordon Lewis's **Free-
dom and Power in the Caribbean** and Julian H. Steward's **The
People of Puerto Rico**. Books cited in other general sections may
contain additional information but the lack of a general subject index
makes their identification difficult and time consuming.

3.036.   Kirschner, Madeline.   **Serving the Spanish Community:
Puerto Rican Bibliography**. Chicago: Adult Services Division, American
Library Association, 1970.

All efforts to locate a copy of this work were unsuccessful. It was
cited in Weinberg, M., **The Education of Poor and Minority
Children** (3.062, vol. 1, p. 501).

3.037.   Lisansky,   Judith.   **Interpersonal   Relations   among
Hispanics in the United States: A Content Analysis of the Social
Science Literature**. Urbana-Champaign, Ill.:   University of Illinois,
Department of Psychology, 1981. 279 p. (Technical Report, 3)

This comprehensive review of the literature deals with Mexicans,
Puerto Ricans and Cubans in the United States. Numerous comparisons
are made among the three groups. The study stresses thought
patterns, basic value orientations, social identification and social
differentiations. It includes references to culture and perceptions of
Anglo society. Scores of references to Puerto Ricans can be found
throughout the report. Works reviewed were judged on a series of
criteria such as field of study, methodology, time frame, characteristics of the sample, and others. Complete bibliographical information is given in the references section at the end of the study.

3.038.   Loeb, Catherine. "The Lives and Politics of Latinas in the United
States: A Selective Bibliography." Madison, Wis.:   The University of
Wisconsin System, 1984. 11 p. (mimeographed)

English-language materials published since 1970 are cited, many with
brief descriptions. Puerto Rican women are included in a special
section of nineteen references, as well as in some works cited in the
general works section.

3.039.   Meadows, Paul. **Recent Immigration to the United States: The Literature of the Social Sciences**. Washington, D.C.: Smithsonian Institution Press, 1976.   112 p.   (RIIES Bibliographic Studies, no. 1) SI 1.40:1.

> An unannotated bibliography which covers the following topics: general migration theory; world immigration trends; impact of immigration on country of origin; impact of immigration on the United States; politics of migration in countries of origin and settlement; settlement process; comparison of old and new immigrants; special relations and background literature on immigration. Scattered references to Puerto Ricans and Puerto Rico are to be found throughout the work although most entries appear under the settlement process.

3.040.   Miller, Wayne Charles. **Comprehensive Bibliography for the study of American Minorities**. 2 vols. New York: New York University Press, 1976.

> A section on Puerto Ricans in the United States can be found on pages 757 to 771 of the second volume. It is introduced by an historical bibliographic essay in which the author asserts that the main reason for Puerto Rican migration was economic, and that most migrants went to New York. Miller also compares the Puerto Rican migrant's experiences to those of other ethnic groups. The problems faced by the migrants are also described, as are the most important sources on the subject. The bibliography is organized in the following sections: bibliographies; organizations; history and sociology; education and language; religion; literature; fiction and autobiography. Author and title indexes included.

3.041.   Momeni, Jamshid A. **Demography of Racial and Ethnic Minorities in the United States: An Annotated Bibliography with a Review Essay**. Westport, Conn.: Greenwood Press, 1984. 292 p.

> Twenty specific references to mainland Puerto Ricans can be found in the minority/subject index. However, many general works on Latin Americans might also prove useful. The emphasis of the bibliography is on social, demographic and health aspects of minorities.

3.042.   Oaks, Priscilla. **Minority Studies: A Selective Annotated Bibliography**. Boston: G. K. Hall, 1975. 303 p.

> Puerto Ricans are one of the minority groups covered in this selective bibliography. Most of the pertinent references are in English. A short

section of bibliographical and reference works is followed by a
section on the general culture and community life of Puerto Ricans
living on the mainland.

3.043.   Ortiz, Ana María. **Bibliography on Hispanic American
History and Culture.** Springfield, Ill.: State Commission on Human
Relations, Department of Education Services, 1972. 25 p. (ED 080 270)

Includes a general bibliography of about fifty items written on or by
Puerto Ricans between 1945 and 1969. Short annotations are given
for the entries which appear in random order. Additional references
can be found in the last section of the work: resources and story
books for children.

3.044.   Padilla, Amado M. and Paul Aranda. **Latino Mental Health:
Bibliography and Abstracts.** Rockville, Md.: U.S. Department of Health,
Education, and Welfare, Public Health Service, Alcohol, Drug Abuse and
Mental Health Administration, National Institute of Mental Health, 1976
(1974). 288 p. (DEW Publication no. ADM 76-317, formerly HSM 73-9144)

An interdisciplinary bibliography, with abstracts, on the mental
health of Latinos in the United States, especially Mexican Americans
and Puerto Ricans. It is arranged alphabetically by author but has a
subject index. Although many of the entries are general in scope,
specific references to Puerto Ricans can be found in the subject index
under "Ethnic groups: Puerto Rican" and under "Puerto Rico." The book
has a separate list of dissertations.

3.045.   Pérez, Nélida and Amílcar Tirado. "Boricuas en el norte."
Revista de Historia 2 (January-June 1986): 128-66.

The history of Pueto Rican migration to the continent is reflected in
this ample bibliographic essay. The compilers discuss the historical
and contemporary literature that has flourished relative to the Puerto
Rican experience: migration, community development, types of migrants, and so forth. Concluding remarks describe the collections of
the Centro de Estudios Puertorriqueños at Hunter College in New York,
and identify other major collections of interest. As an appendix to
the essay, three valuable bibliographies are included: a bibliography
of 21 bibliographies on Puerto Ricans in the United States; a selective
bibliography on Puerto Ricans in the United States; and a preliminary
list of microfilm (eleven journals and newspapers) on the Puerto
Rican community in New York. An important and comprehensive
contribution.

3.046.   [Pérez, Nélida and Tirado, Amílcar]. "Boricuas en el Norte: A Selected Bibliography on Puerto Ricans in the United States." In **Latin American Masses and Minorities: Their Images and Realities**, edited by Seminar on the Acquisition of Latin American Library Materials (30th: 1985: Princeton, N.J.), vol. 2, 556-61. Madison, Wisc.: SALALM Secretariat , 1987.

> Authorship is not specified in the publication but can easily be identified as part 2 of the article of the same title published in **Revista de Historia** (3.045).

3.047..   **The Puerto Ricans: Migration and General Bibliography**. New York: Arno Press, 1975. 1 vol (various pagings)

> This collection reprints the following bibliographies, each with its original pagination: Clarence Senior's **A Selected Bibliography on Puerto Rico and the Puerto Ricans** (1951); Senior's **Bibliography on Puerto Ricans in the United States** (1959); Francesco Cordasco's **The People of Puerto Rico** (1968); **Puerto Rican Migrants on the Mainland of the United States** (IRCD **Bulletin**, January 1968); Frank Cordasco and Leonard Covello's **Studies of Puerto Rican Children in American Schools (Journal of Human Relations**, 1968); Jesse Dossick's **Doctoral Research on Puerto Rico and Puerto Ricans** (1967); A.P.C. Griffin's **A List of Books, with References to Periodicals on Porto Rico** (1901). Each of these is annotated separately under author throughout the present work.

3.048.   San Diego County Board of Education.   **A Multicultural Bibliography**. San Diego, Calif.: 1976. 77 p. (ED 211 658)

> There are eighteen entries for works of fiction dealing with a Puerto Rican theme. However, only one work was written by a Puerto Rican. Short plot descriptions are given as is the educational level of each item.

3.049.   Sánchez, George I. and Howard Putman. **Materials Relating to the Education of Spanish-Speaking People in the United States**. Austin, Tex.: The Institute of Latin American Studies, 1959. 76 p.

> Although only nine references deal specifically with Puerto Rico, many general works could also contain informantion relevant to the education of mainland Puerto Ricans.

3.050.   Sanua, Víctor D. "Immigration, Migration and Mental Illness: A
Review of the Literature with Special Emphasis on Schizophrenia."   In
Behavior in New Environments: Adaptation of Migrant Populations,
edited by Eugene B. Brody, 291-352. Beverly Hills, Calif.: Sage Publications,
1970.

> This extended bibliographic essay includes a section on Puerto Ricans
> on the mainland with explanations of the theories set forth in each
> study. Comparisons of the patterns and rates of mental illness among
> Puerto Ricans are made with that of other migrant groups.

3.051.   Schwartz, Eleanor E. "On the Mainland: A Look at Pueto Ricans
in America as Seen in Current Media" **NJEA Review** 52 (November 1978):
40-41.

> This brief bibliographical essay describes approximately twenty-
> three items which discuss or illustrate the Puerto Rican experience in
> the continental United States. Most are English-language sources.

3.052.   Senior, Clarence, ed. **Bibliography on Puerto Ricans in the
United States**. New York: 1959. 37 p.

> Focusing on migration and the situation of Puerto Ricans on the
> mainland, this partially annotated bibliography cites books, reports
> and government documents, and newspaper and magazine articles. The
> main section covers up to December of 1958. An appendix adds
> materials published from January 1 to April 30, 1959. This is one of
> the most frequently cited bibliographies relating to Puerto Ricans on
> the mainland. (Also published in **The Puerto Ricans: Migration
> and General Bibliography**. New York: Arno Press, 1975.)

3.053.   **Sourcebook of Hispanic Culture in the United States**.
Edited by David William Foster. Chicago: American Library Association,
1982. 352 p.

> Three major groups are studied: Mexican Americans, Puerto Ricans
> and Cuban Americans. The section on continental Puerto Ricans (pages
> 133 to 200) is subdivided into four parts, each with an introductory
> essay followed by an annotated bibliography. Teresita Martínez de
> Carrerá and Julio Ramos prepared the first part on the history of the
> Puerto Rican experience on the mainland and return migration. Their
> essay is followed by a bibliography of twenty-eight items. Ronald J.
> Duncan is responsible for the anthropology and sociology sections in
> which he traces the evolution of each discipline on the island. Each of
> the bibliographies describes twenty-eight studies. The art section,

written by Catharine E. Wall, considers the relationship of Puerto Rican continental art to its island counterpart, and briefly traces its evolution. Thirty-five items are annotated. The literature, education, sociolinguistics and music of the Cuban Americans and Puerto Ricans are dealt with jointly in a chapter entitled "General". Author and title indexes are included in this important work.

3.054.   Sowell, Thomas. **Bibliographic Index of American Ethnic Groups**. 2 vols. Washington, D.C.: Urban Institute,[1976] 681 p. (ED 129 708)

Volume two contains a substantial section of citations relating to all aspects of the Puerto Rican experience on the mainland. Arranged by topic, references are given to the pages in books and articles where relevant information is to be found. "The kind of literature preferred for this index was empirically based, factual and analytical material, in contrast to moral, ideological, dramatic or romantic approaches to American ethnicity."

3.055.   Techner, Richard V., D. Garland and Jerry R. Craddock. **Spanish and English of United States Hispanics: A Critical Annotated Linguistic Bibliography**. Arlington, Va.: Center for Applied Linguistics, 1975. 352 p.

An annotated bibliography on the speech and language behavior of Hispanics in the United States. Among the introductory essays can be found one on Puerto Rican Spanish. A chapter on Puerto Ricans on the mainland (pages 258-301) has the following subtopics: bibliography, general/comprehensive studies and anthologies; festschriften; sociolinguistics; textbooks; Spanish phonology; Spanish grammar; lexicon; influence of English on Spanish; English of Puerto Ricans.

3.056.   United States. Cabinet Committee on Opportunities for the Spanish Speaking People. **The Spanish Speaking in the United States: A Guide to Materials** With a new foreword by Francesco Cordasco. Washington, D.C.: 1971; Detroit: Blaine Ethridge, 1975. 175 p.

Although the emphasis is on the Mexican American community, this book does include material on Puerto Rico and Puerto Ricans. These may be found by consulting the index. Includes print and non-print items.

3.057.   University of Michigan. Center for Afroamerican and African Studies. **Black Immigration and Ethnicity in the United States: An**

Annotated Bibliography. Westport, Conn.: Greenwood Press, 1985. 170 p.

> Covers Black immigration "of recent decades" and its effects on the American Black population. The first chapter is a bibliography of bibliographies and literature surveys. A section on Puerto Ricans in the United States can be found on pages 117 to 144. Many annotations are included. Author and subject indexes add to the value of this work.

3.058.   Valverde, Leonard A., Rosa Castro Feinberg, and Esther M. Marquez. **Educating English-Speaking Hispanics**.   Alexandria, Va.: Association for Supervision and Curriculum Development, 1980. 98 p. (ED 197 908)

> Following chapters which discuss curriculum concerns and instructional techniques for use with Hispanic children who speak English only, annotated bibliographies focus on different Latino groups. The section on Puerto Ricans was prepared by Ramón L. Santiago. He provides references and annotations for eleven books on history and culture, nineteen which deal with "contributors to present society"; and sixteen for imaginative literature. Six references are also given to journals and encyclopedias. All sections cover both Puerto Rico and Puerto Ricans on the mainland.

3.059.   Velázquez, René. **Puerto Ricans in Continental United States: A Bibliography, Selected and Annotated**. New York: City College of the City University of New York [1975] 146 p. (ED 189 207)

> Almost 900 books, newspaper and journal articles and theses are described in this work. An excellent section of bibliographies precedes the main alphabetical listing of works on Puerto Ricans in the United States. Some general works on Puerto Rico are also included. Emphasizes social, psychological, economic and educational studies.

3.060.   Vivó, Paquita. **Puerto Rican Migration: The Return Flow. La migración puertorriqueña: el reflujo a la isla** Washington, D.C.: National Institute of Education, 1982. 161 p. (ED 221 635)

> As well as describing the book's organization, the introduction includes general observations and conclusions on the literature of the topic, and comments on available statistical sources. The annotated entries are grouped alphabetically under the following headings: books, journal articles and printed documents; doctoral dissertations; journalistic accounts; and unpublished materials. Masters theses are

not annotated. An appendix lists names and addresses of individuals and groups who are doing research on return migration or wish to be informed of accomplishments in that area. An author index completes the work. This is an important work by an authoritative compiler. It may be used with the Carrasquillo bibliography (3.011).

3.061.   Washington (State). Department of Education. **Listing of Resource Material Concerned with the Spanish Speaking**. Olympia, Wash.: Superintendent of Instruction, 1971. 1 vol.

A short bibliography of books for Hispanics and materials on the Spanish-speaking in general. Puerto Ricans are included.

3.062.   Weinberg, Meyer. **The Education of Poor and Minority Children: A World Bibliography**. 2 vols. Westport, Conn.: Greenwood Press, 1981. (1563 p.)

While the emphasis of this work is on schooling, "matters such as economic equality and inequality, racism and antiracism, class structure, ethnic organization, and other influential factors bearing on education are also covered in depth." The bibliography is arranged by general subjects divided into subtopics. At the end of each major section a useful bibliography of bibliographies is included. The main section on Puerto Ricans can be found on pages 475 to 490 of volume one. Author index.

3.063.   _____. **The Education of the Minority Child: A Comprehensive Bibliography of 10,000 Selected Entries**. Chicago: Integrated Education Associates, 1970. 530 p.

Emphasizing the last seventy years, this unannotated bibliography deals with the education of Puerto Rican children as well as those of other minority groups. Arranged by subject with an author index. Includes bibliographies.

3.064.   Wilgus, Karna S. **Latin America Books: An Annotated Bibliography for High Schools and Colleges**. New York: Center for Inter-American Relations, 1974. 80 p.

This selective, annotated bibliography of English-language sources has a section on Puerto Rico and Puerto Ricans in the United States (pages 50 to 52). It is divided into two parts: books for students, and materials for teachers and general references. Somewhat dated.

3.065.   Zirkel, Perry A. **Puerto Rican Pupils: A Bibliography.**
Hartford, Conn.: University of Hartford, College of Education, 1973. 61 p.

This unannotated list is intended to be of help to teachers and others
interested in improving educational opportunities for Puerto Rican
children, both on the island and on the mainland. Entries are grouped
under the following headings: English books on Puerto Rican culture;
Spanish books on Puerto Rican culture; children's literature; audio-
visual materials; "self-contained research studies"; journal articles;
and bibliographies. Some items listed as bibliographies do not really
qualify as such. No indexes.

Author Index

Title Index

Arquitectura para el trópico, 2.010

Articles on Puerto Rico from **La Torre**, 1.012

Artículos científicos en América Latina 1950, 2.305

Background books: Puerto Rico, 1.008

Bibliografía, 2.019, 2.107

Bibliografía actual del Caribe, 1.037

Bibliografía acumulativa, 2.336

Bibliografía americanista española, 1935-1963, 2.116

Bibliografía anotada Colección Domingo Toledo Alamo, 2.181

Bibliografía anotada de artículos acerca de la juventud, 2.337

Bibliografía anotada de la música en Puerto Rico, 2.006

Bibliografía anotada de preescolares, 2.108

Bibliografía anotada: revistas y periódicos de Puerto Rico en el siglo XIX, 1.101

Bibliografía anotada sobre los recursos humanos, 2.074

Bibliografía anotada sobre Myrna Baez, 2.035

Bibliografía antropológica para el estudio de los pueblos indígenas en el Caribe, 2.331

Bibliografía básica para la historia de Puerto Rico, 2.162

Bibliografía bibliotecológica, 2.186

Bibliografía comentada sobre la pesca y las localidades pesqueras en Puerto Rico, 2.274

Bibliografía cultural de Puerto Rico, 1.065

Bibliografía de antropología física en el Caribe, 2.325

Bibliografía de artículos escritos por Don Miguel Meléndez Muñoz para **Puerto Rico Ilustrado** de

1910-1952, 2.028

Bibliografía de asuntos juveniles en Puerto Rico, 2.327

Bibliografía de bibliografías del Caribe, 1.004

Bibliografía de Carlos Méndez Santos, 1959-1979, 2.048

Bibliografía de Centro América y del Caribe, 1.013

Bibliografía de Concha Meléndez, 2.026

Bibliografía de educación en Puerto Rico, 2.098

Bibliografía de Emilio Díaz Valcarcel, 2.033

Bibliografía [de Emilio S. Belaval], 2.043

Bibliografía de escritores hispanoamericanos, 2.196

Bibliografía de Ester Feliciano Mendoza, 2.014

Bibliografía de Eugenio María de Hostos, 2.022

Bibliografía de fuentes estadísticas escogidas de las naciones americanas, 2.358

Bibliografía de J. Benjamín Torres, 2.023

Bibliografía de José Luis González, 2.062

Bibliografía de la huelga universitaria de 1981, 2.100

Bibliografía de la lingüística española, 2.174

Bibliografía de la mujer, 2.353

Bibliografía de la música, 2.009

Bibliografía de la promoción del '70, 2.224

Bibliografía de libros sobre la mujer en Puerto Rico, 2.345

Bibliografía de Luis Palés Matos, 2.070, 2.024

Bibliografía de Margot Arce de Vázquez, 2.018

Bibliografía de Manuel Zeno Gandía,

Subject Index

About the Compiler

FAY FOWLIE-FLORES is Librarian III and Director, Office of Planning and Institutional Research, University of Puerto Rico, Ponce. Her previous publications include *Ponce: Perla del Sur; una bibliografia anotada* (1988) and *Index to Puerto Rican Collective Biography* (Greenwood Press, 1987) among others.

www.ingramcontent.com/pod-product-compliance
Lightning Source LLC
Chambersburg PA
CBHW021540260326
41914CB00001B/99